SKYSCRAPERS

The Heights of Engineering

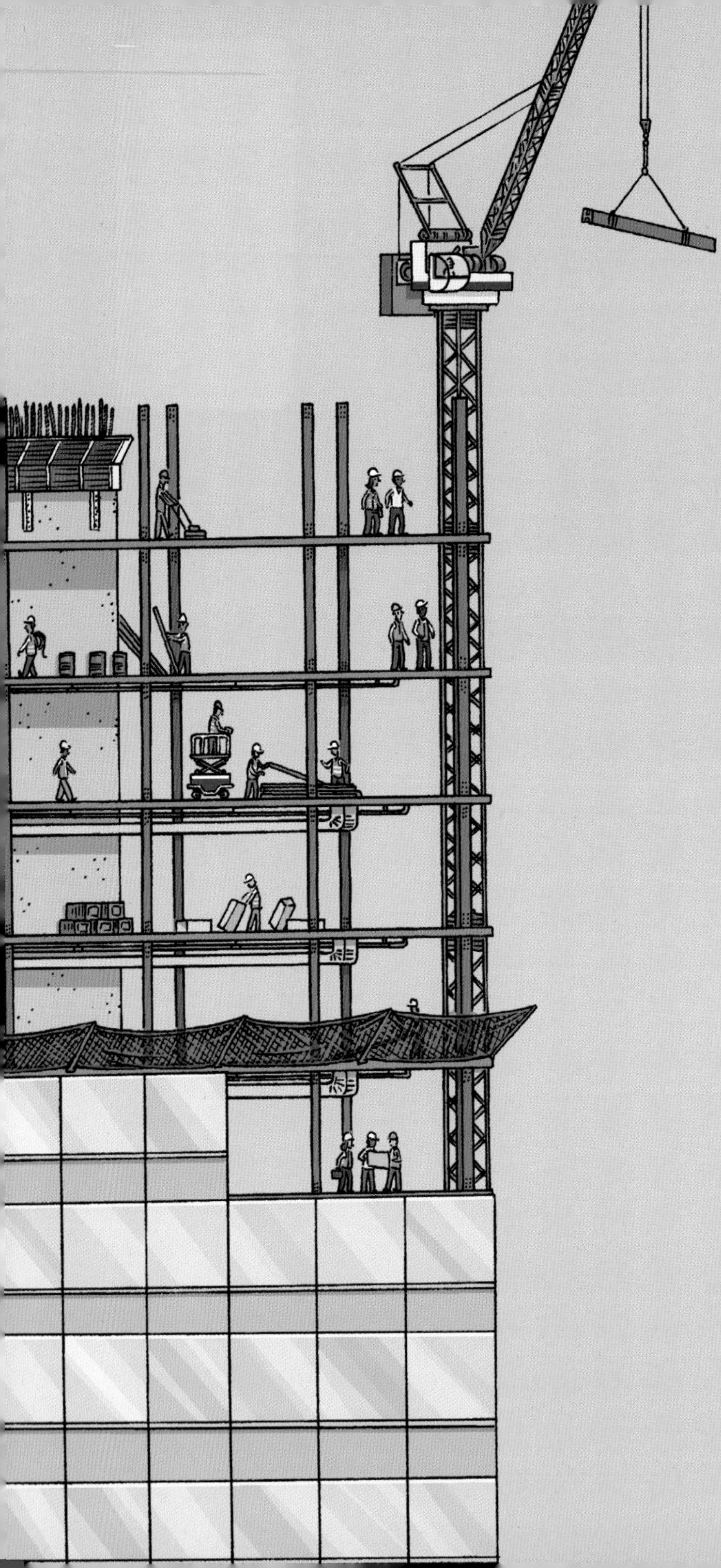

SKYSCRAPERS

The Heights of Engineering

John Kerschbaum

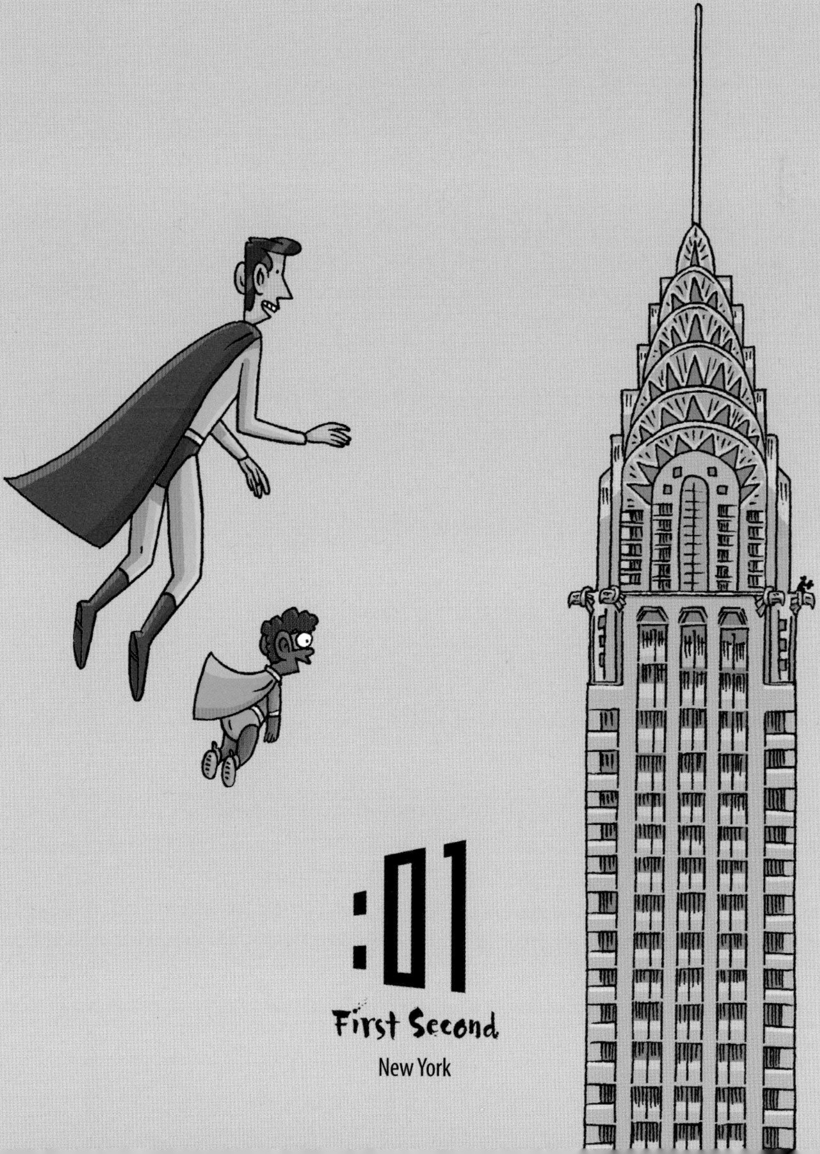

:01
First Second
New York

For Frances and Norah

First Second

Published by First Second
First Second is an imprint of Roaring Brook Press,
a division of Holtzbrinck Publishing Holdings Limited Partnership
120 Broadway, New York, NY 10271

Don't miss your next favorite book from First Second! For the latest updates
go to firstsecondnewsletter.com and sign up for our enewsletter.

Library of Congress Control Number: 2018953663

Paperback ISBN: 978-1-62672-794-6
Hardcover ISBN: 978-1-62672-795-3

Our books may be purchased in bulk for promotional, educational, or business use. Please contact your local bookseller or the Macmillan Corporate and Premium Sales Department at (800) 221-7945 ext. 5442 or by email at MacmillanSpecialMarkets@macmillan.com.

FIRST EDITION

First edition, 2019
Edited by Dave Roman
Skyscraper consultant: Donald Friedman, PE, F.APT, F.ASCE
Cover design by Andrew Arnold and Chris Dickey
Interior book design by Rob Steen
Printed in China by Toppan Leefung Printing Ltd., Dongguan City, Guangdong Province

Drawn with Derwent 2H and H pencils on Strathmore 100-lb. Bristol. Inked with various sized Pigma Micron pens. Corrections were made with Copic Opaque White applied with a ten-year-old Winsor & Newton Series 7 watercolor brush, size 00, that has only about a dozen hairs left in it. The art was then scanned and colored in Photoshop.

10 9 8 7 6 5

BY ART WE LIVE

Since the dawn of mankind, people have dreamed of reaching the sky. Early civilizations built colossal monuments like the Great Pyramids of Giza and the Yongning Temple in China to showcase their great achievements. And while much has changed since the days of the ancient Egyptians, humanity's desire to build higher has only grown. Even today, cities compete to build ever-taller buildings as a sign of their importance and to mark their arrival on the world stage. Yet the massive skyscrapers of the modern world are more than just monuments—they're one of the keys to ensuring that we keep the Earth healthy and habitable for generations to come.

As the world's population continues to grow, more and more people will need to fit into the same amount of space that we have today; the Earth isn't getting any bigger, after all. In fact, the first skyscrapers were built to accommodate the great migration of people to cities like New York and Chicago during the Industrial Revolution around 1760–1830. Since then, skyscrapers have sprouted all over the globe as people flock to urban centers in search of better opportunities. With more people living and working in tall buildings, there's more room for farmers to grow their crops and less of a need to cut down forests to make way for human development.

And recently, the trend of people moving to cities to live and work in tall buildings has only accelerated. Each year, the Council on Tall Buildings and Urban Habitat studies the number of skyscrapers taller than 656 feet (200 meters) that are built. In 2008, there were 47 such skyscrapers completed; in 2017, that number jumped to a record-breaking 144 completions.

Not only are we building more skyscrapers, but these buildings continue to get taller and taller as well. Faster, more powerful elevators have allowed builders to grow their towers to new heights by transporting people hundreds of feet in the air in a matter of seconds. Technical advances in engineering have also made tall buildings more structurally sound. These factors, among others, have led to a seemingly endless competition to build the world's tallest building.

At the beginning of the 21st century, the Petronas Twin Towers in Kuala Lumpur held the title of world's tallest buildings, rising 1,483 ft (452 m) above the ground. In 2004, Taipei 101 in Taiwan took their crown, standing roughly 164 ft (50 m) taller than the Petronas Towers. By 2010, the Burj Khalifa in Dubai had taken the top spot—climbing to an incredible 2,719 ft (828 m). Yet the competition is far from over. Today, an even taller tower is being built in Jeddah, Saudi Arabia, that is expected to top out at 3,281 ft (1,000 m) above the Earth.

Looking toward the future, skyscrapers will continue to evolve in fascinating ways. We're just now beginning to see the implementation of skybridges—which connect tall buildings hundreds of feet in the air and allow cities to form new networks high above the ground. These "horizontal" skyscrapers are being made possible by inventions such as a new type of elevator that goes side to side as well as up and down.

New technologies are also making buildings smarter, allowing them to learn from their daily interactions with humans and provide services based on this information. As we speak, the newest generation of skyscrapers is helping to reduce the greenhouse gases that cause climate change by, for example, admitting optimal sunlight to reduce the need for artificial light.

These innovations—among many others—will dramatically change how cities look and operate in the near future. Around 2.5 billion people will be added to the world's cities by 2050, so it's important that we continue to think of new and creative ways for our cities to grow taller, smarter, and more connected. Clearly, skyscrapers are not simply a passing trend or a way for cities to boast their statuses; they are the future of humanity on our planet.

With your help, we can build the next generation of smart, sustainable cities. But first, explore the history and the inner workings of tall buildings with this dynamically illustrated introduction to skyscrapers!

—Antony Wood, Executive Director of the
Council on Tall Buildings and Urban Habitat

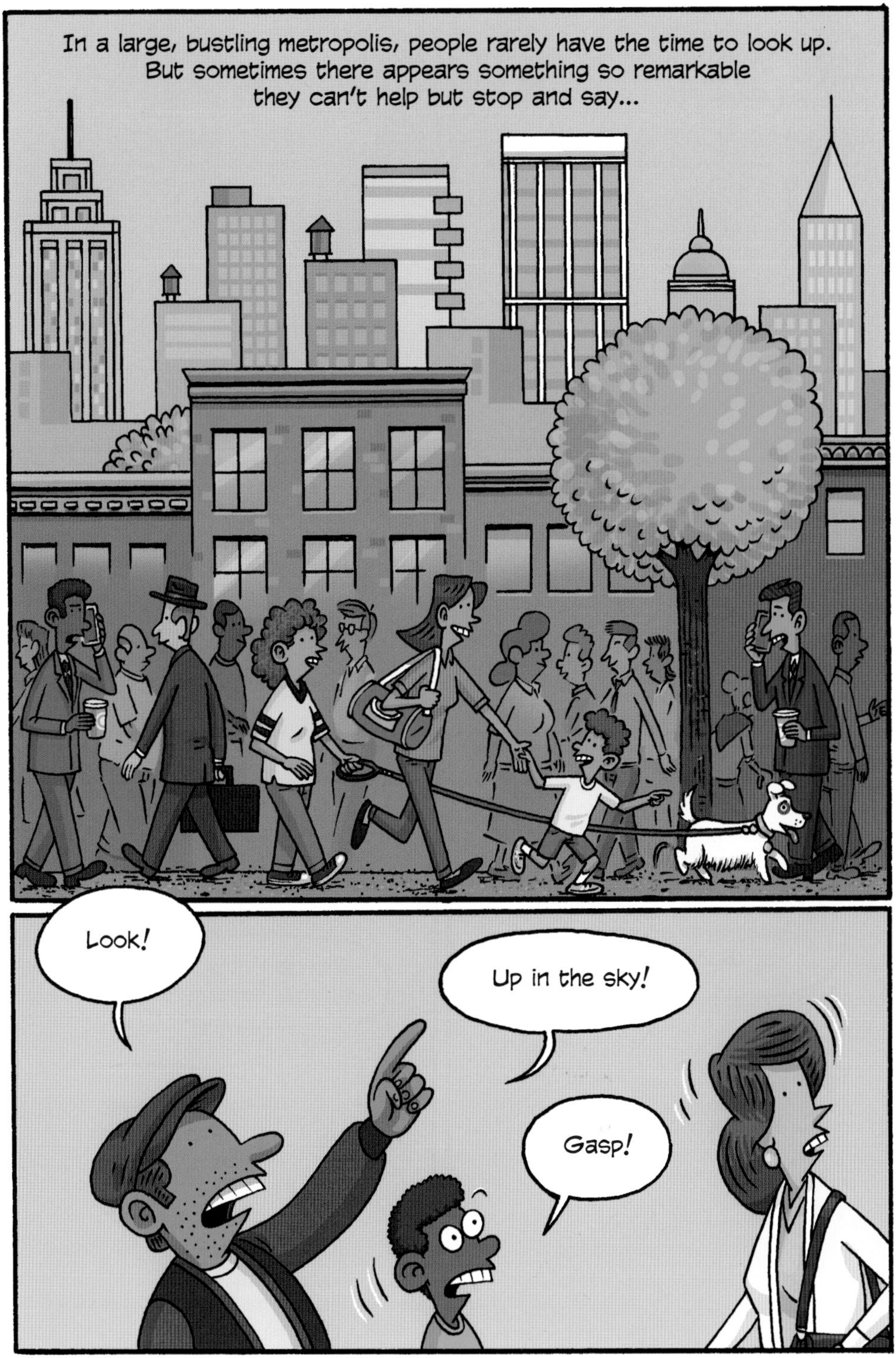
In a large, bustling metropolis, people rarely have the time to look up. But sometimes there appears something so remarkable they can't help but stop and say...
Look!
Up in the sky!
Gasp!

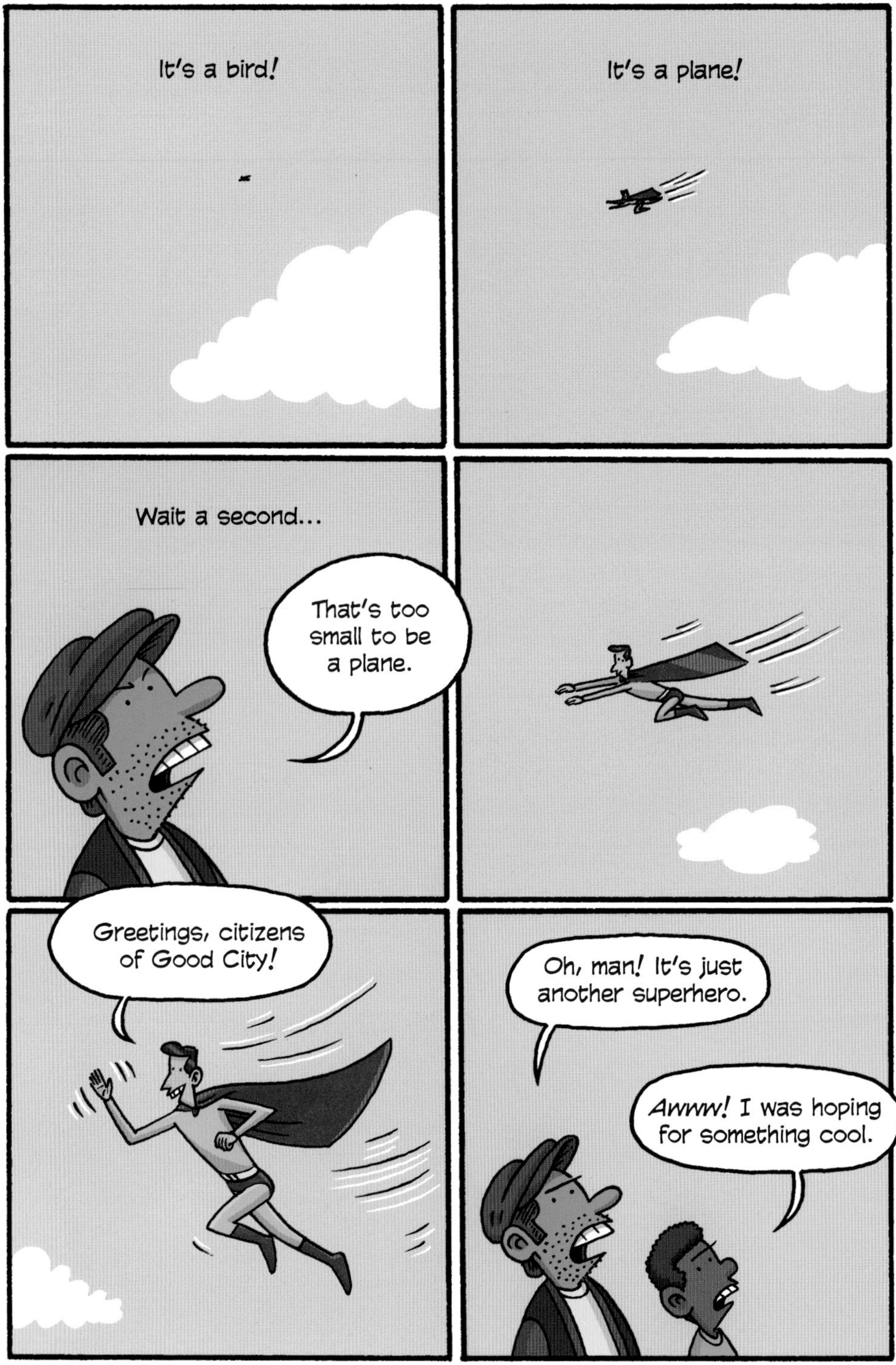
It's a bird!
It's a plane!
Wait a second...
That's too small to be a plane.
Greetings, citizens of Good City!
Oh, man! It's just another superhero.
Awww! I was hoping for something cool.

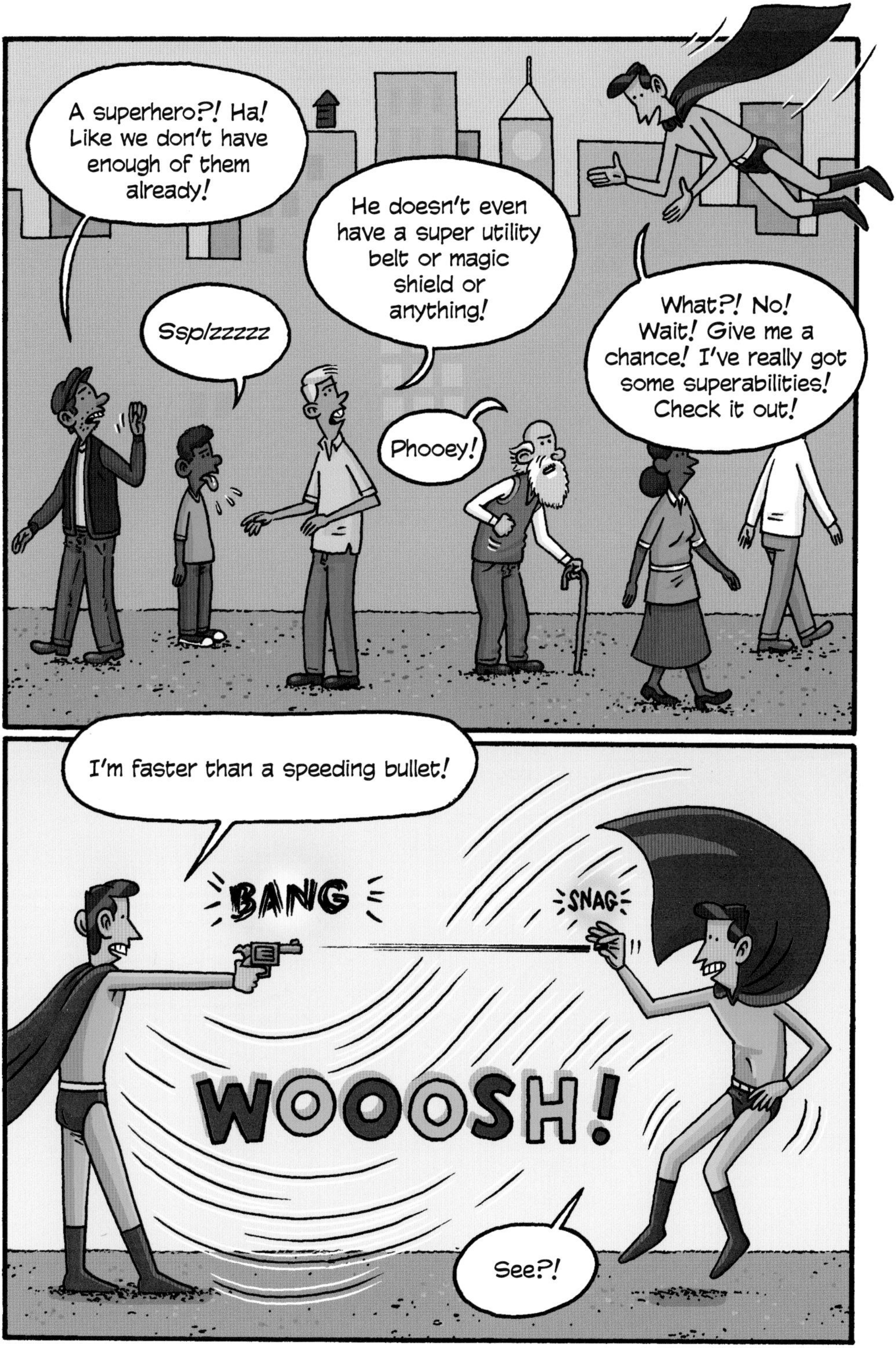
A superhero?! Ha! Like we don't have enough of them already!
Ssplzzzzz
He doesn't even have a super utility belt or magic shield or anything!
Phooey!
What?! No! Wait! Give me a chance! I've really got some superabilities! Check it out!
I'm faster than a speeding bullet!
BANG
SNAG
WOOOSH!
See?!

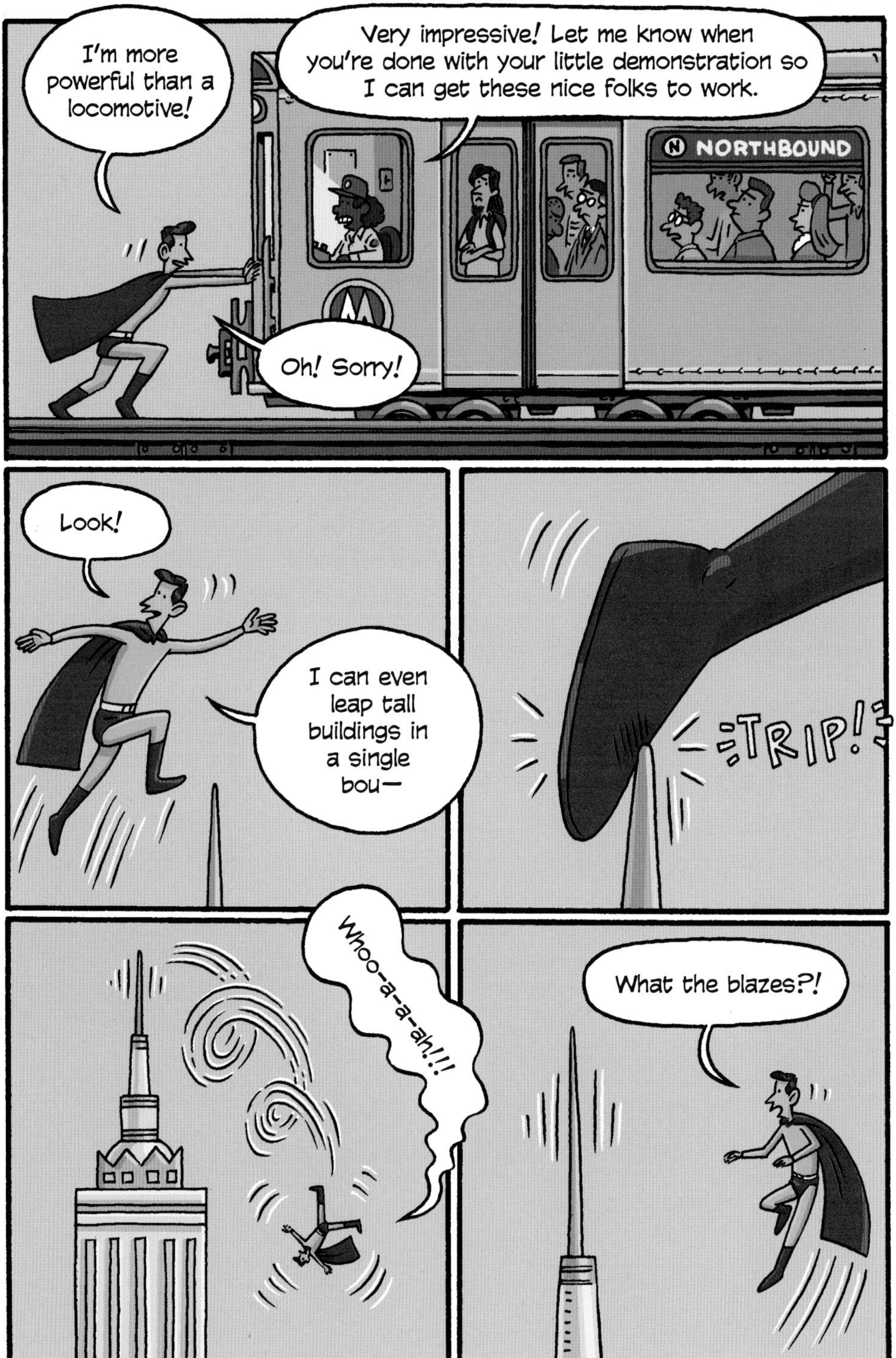

I'm more powerful than a locomotive!
Very impressive! Let me know when you're done with your little demonstration so I can get these nice folks to work.
NORTHBOUND
Oh! Sorry!
Look!
I can even leap tall buildings in a single bou—
TRIP!
Whoo-a-a-ah!!!
What the blazes?!

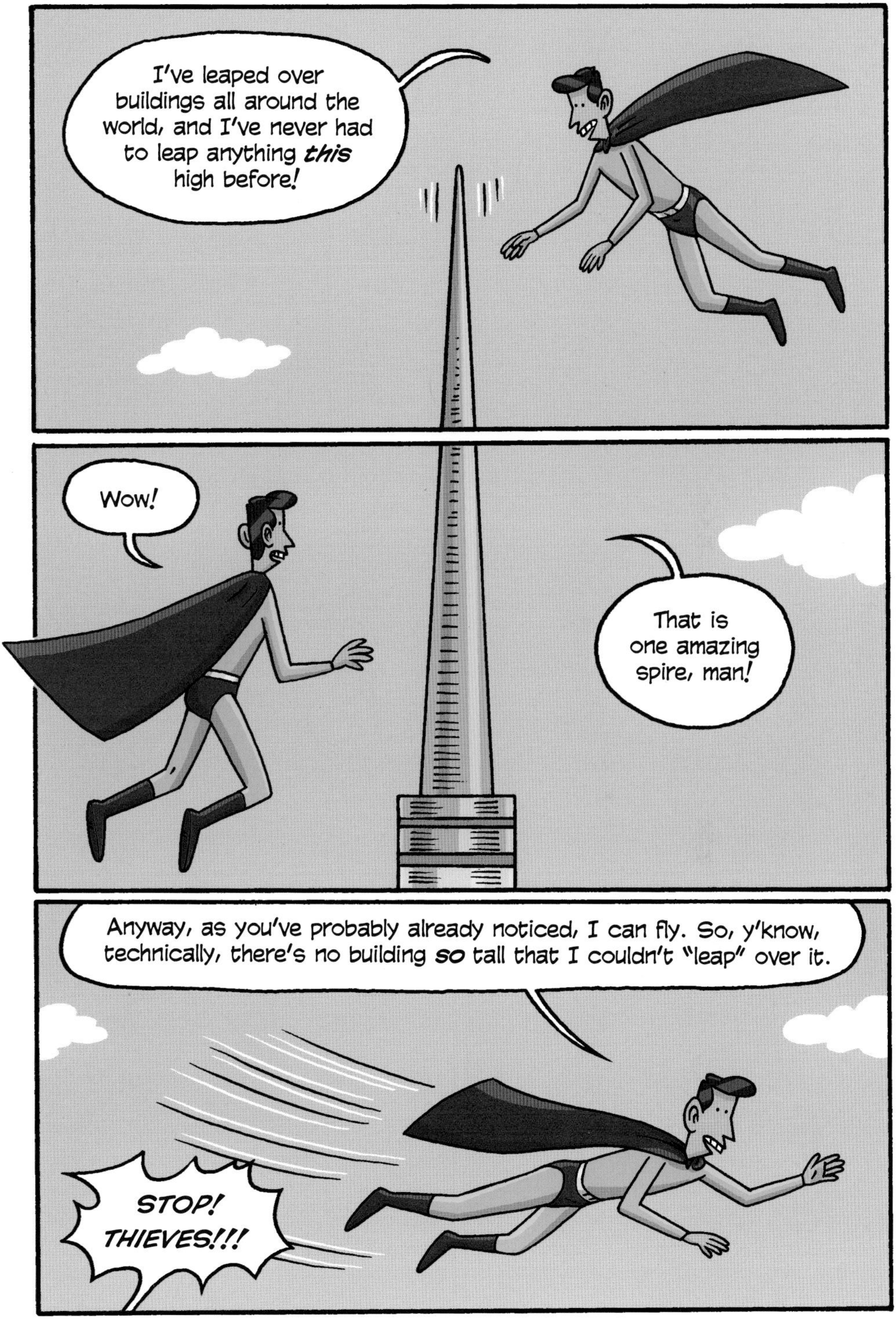
I've leaped over buildings all around the world, and I've never had to leap anything *this* high before!
Wow!
That is one amazing spire, man!
Anyway, as you've probably already noticed, I can fly. So, y'know, technically, there's no building *so* tall that I couldn't "leap" over it.
STOP! THIEVES!!!

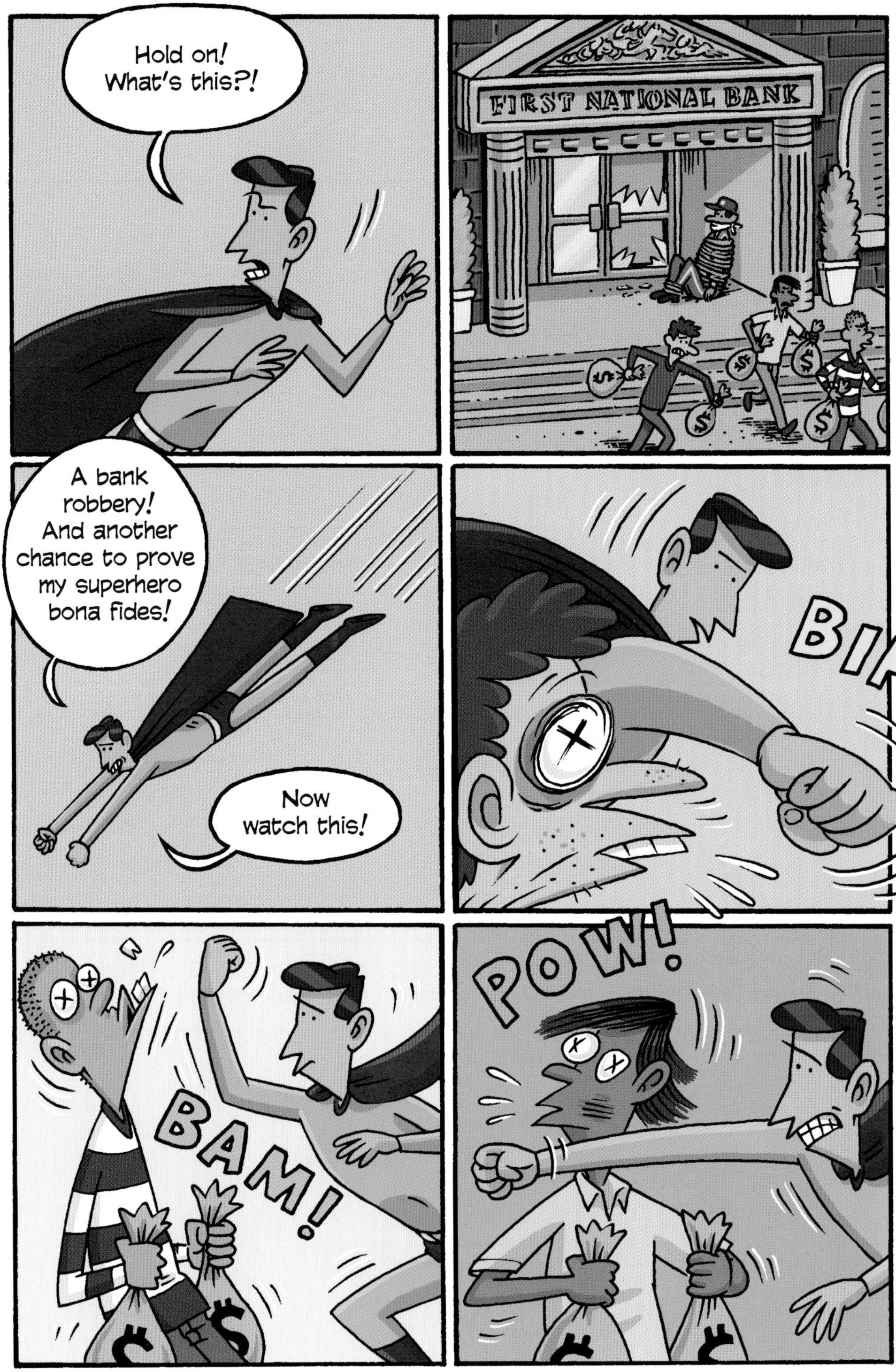

Hold on! What's this?!
FIRST NATIONAL BANK
A bank robbery! And another chance to prove my superhero bona fides!
Now watch this!
BIF!
BAM!
POW!

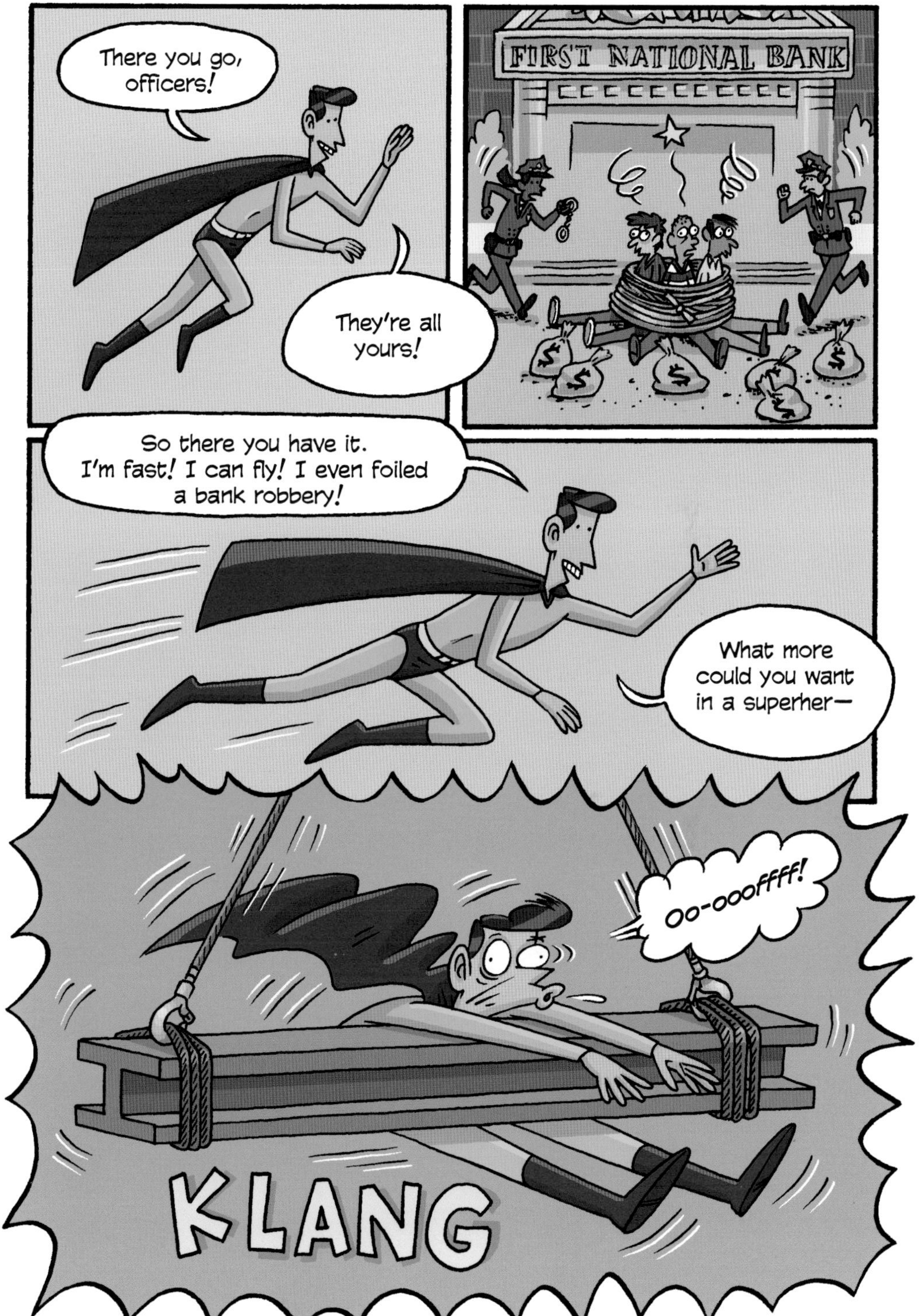
There you go, officers!
They're all yours!
FIRST NATIONAL BANK
So there you have it. I'm fast! I can fly! I even foiled a bank robbery!
What more could you want in a superher—
Oo-oooffff!
KLANG

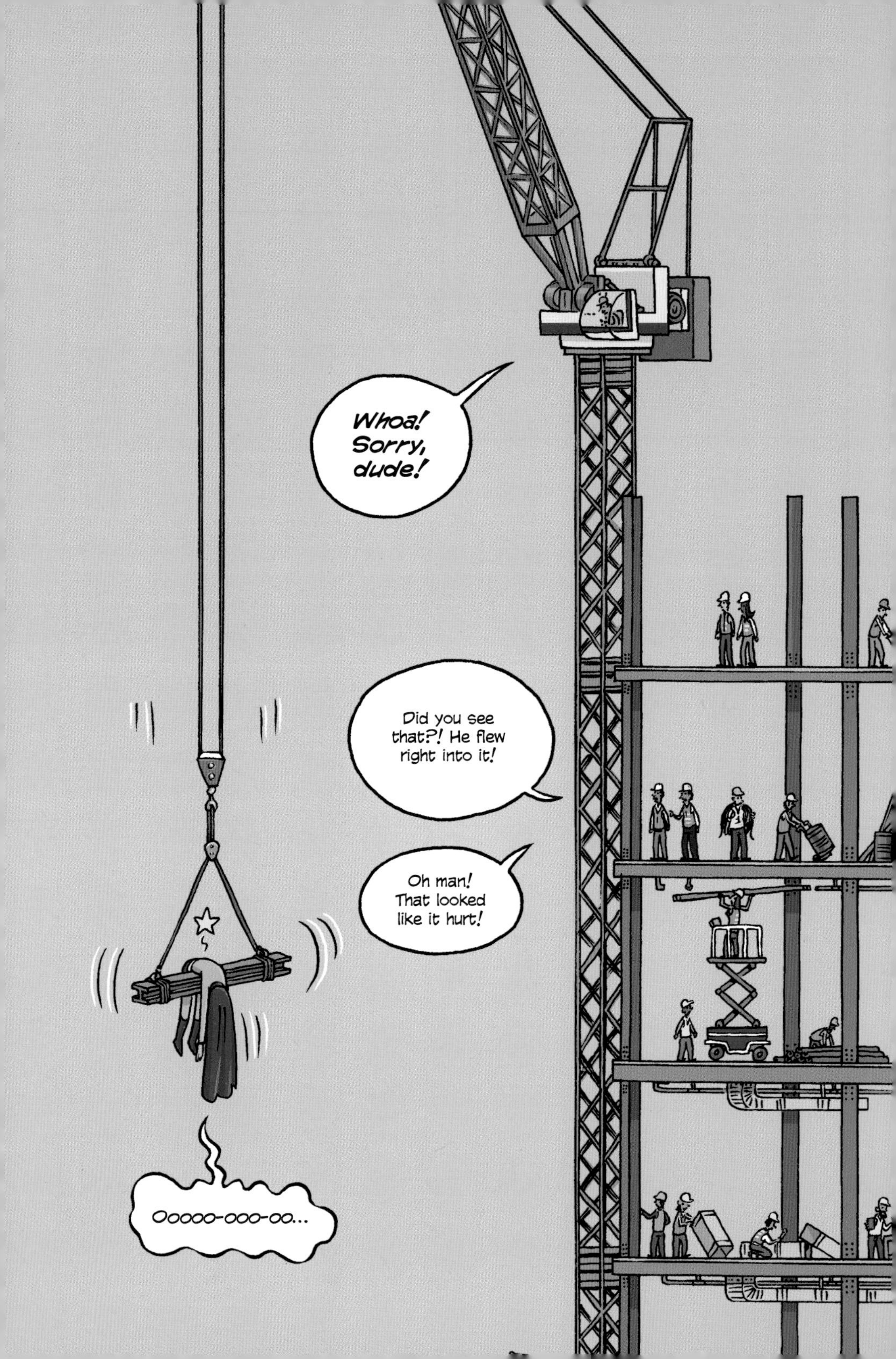
Whoa! Sorry, dude!
Did you see that?! He flew right into it!
Oh man! That looked like it hurt!
Ooooo-ooo-oo...

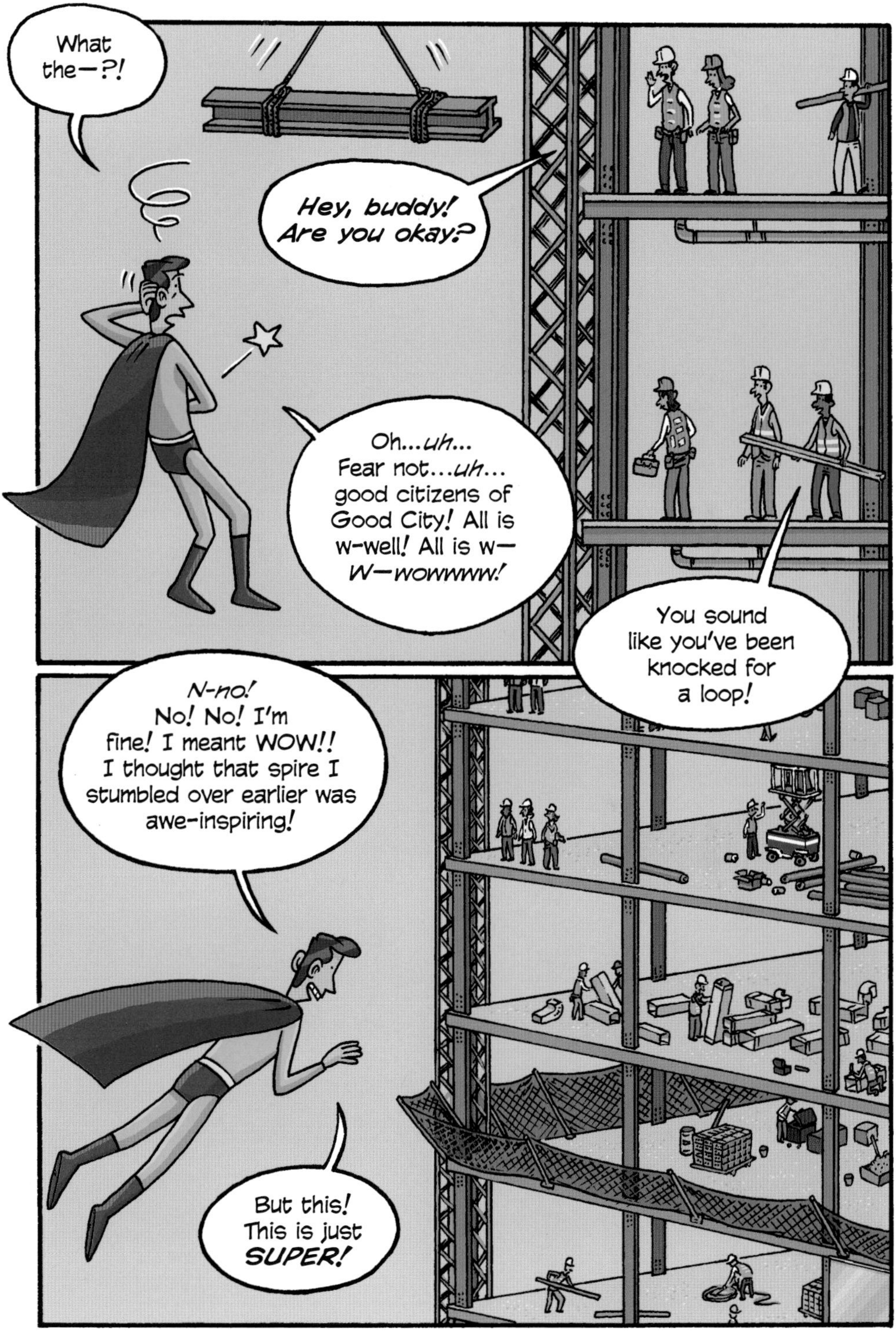
What the—?!
Hey, buddy! Are you okay?
Oh...uh... Fear not...uh... good citizens of Good City! All is w-well! All is w— W—wowwww!
You sound like you've been knocked for a loop!
N-no! No! No! I'm fine! I meant WOW!! I thought that spire I stumbled over earlier was awe-inspiring!
But this! This is just SUPER!

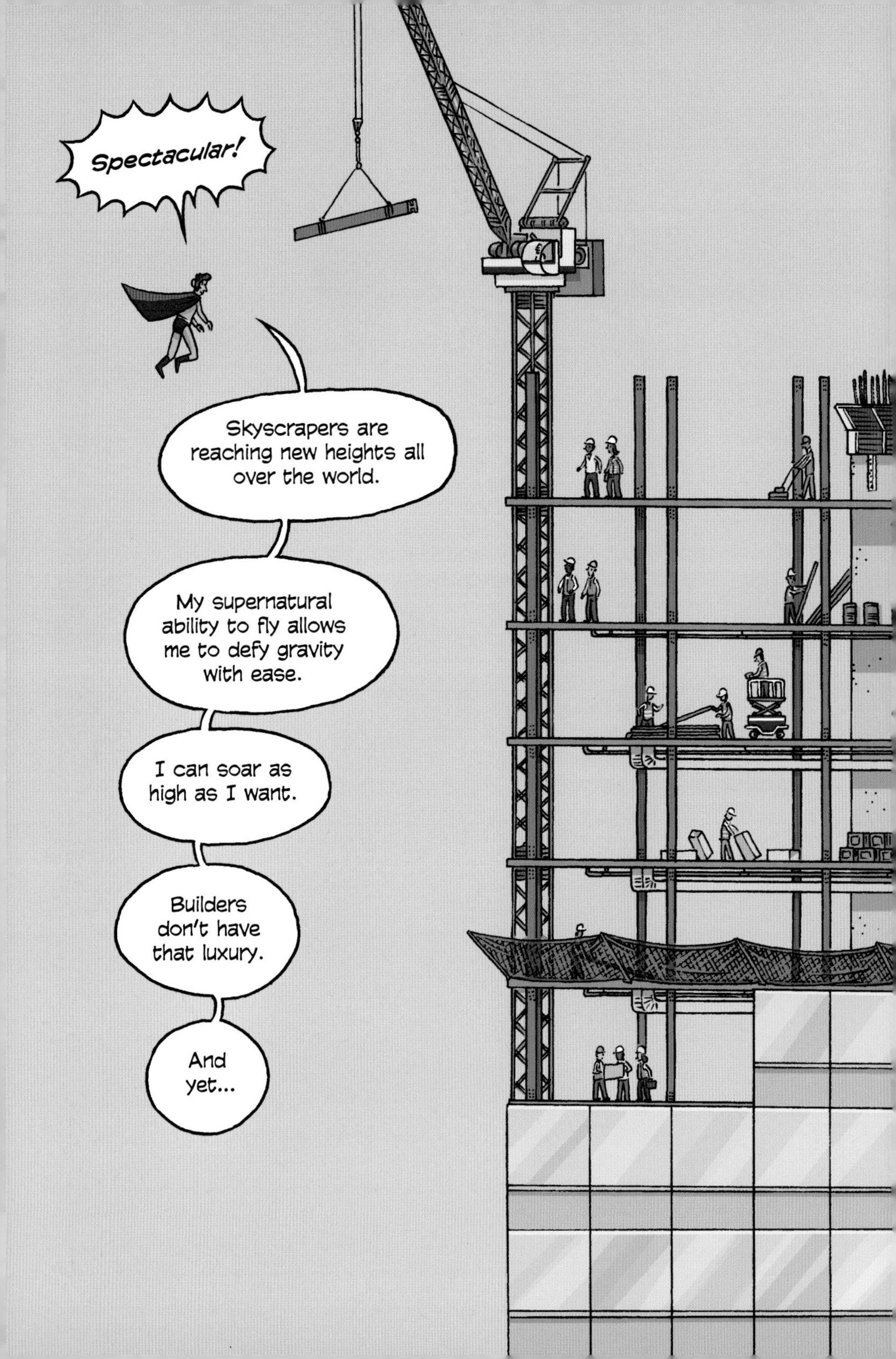
Spectacular!
Skyscrapers are reaching new heights all over the world.
My supernatural ability to fly allows me to defy gravity with ease.
I can soar as high as I want.
Builders don't have that luxury.
And yet...

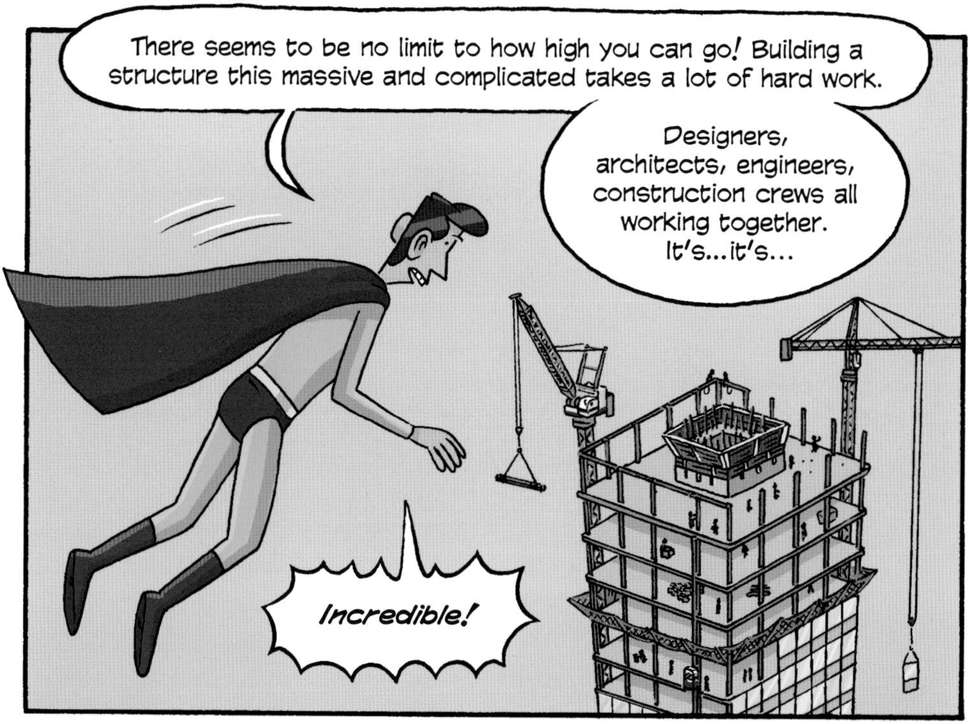
There seems to be no limit to how high you can go! Building a structure this massive and complicated takes a lot of hard work.
Designers, architects, engineers, construction crews all working together. It's...it's...
Incredible!

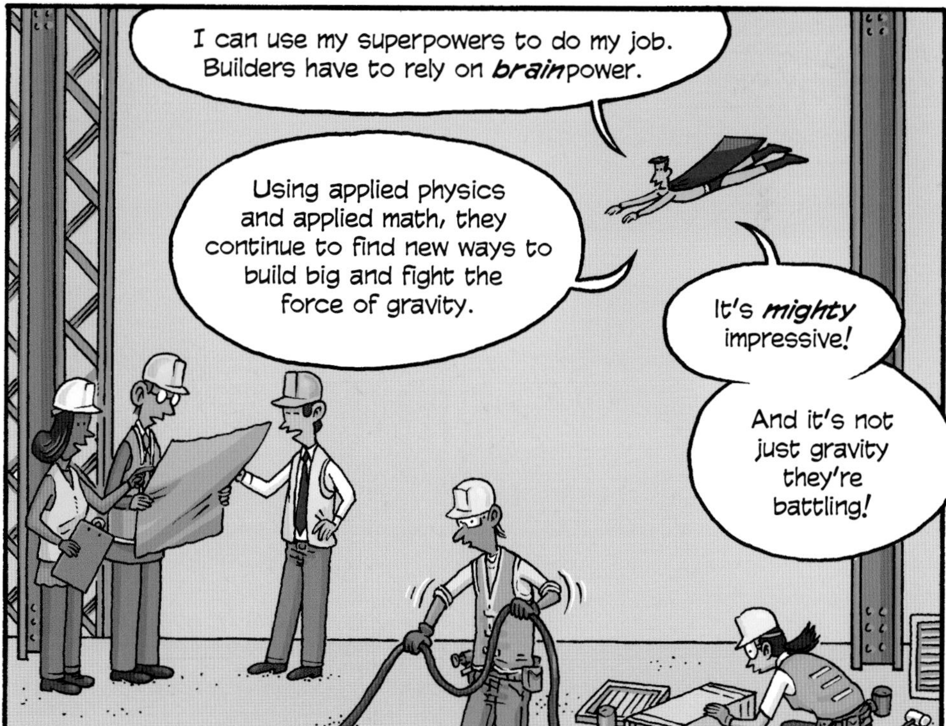
I can use my superpowers to do my job. Builders have to rely on brainpower.
Using applied physics and applied math, they continue to find new ways to build big and fight the force of gravity.
It's mighty impressive!
And it's not just gravity they're battling!

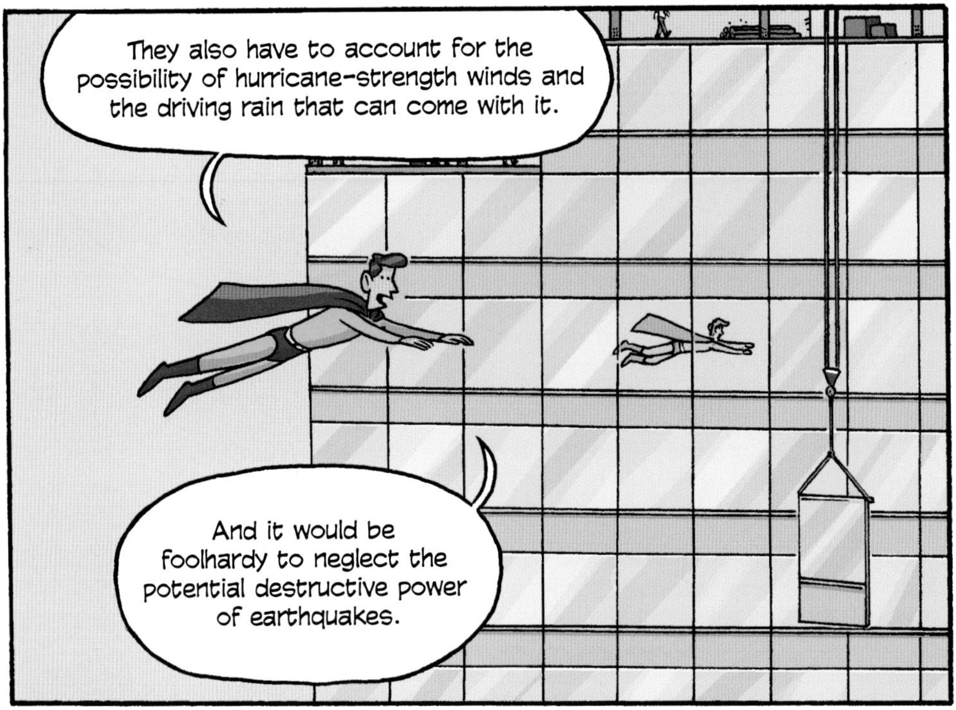
They also have to account for the possibility of hurricane-strength winds and the driving rain that can come with it.
And it would be foolhardy to neglect the potential destructive power of earthquakes.

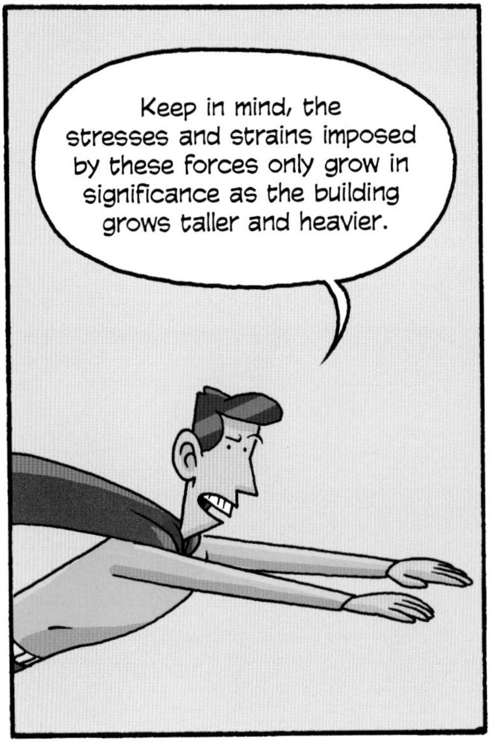
Keep in mind, the stresses and strains imposed by these forces only grow in significance as the building grows taller and heavier.

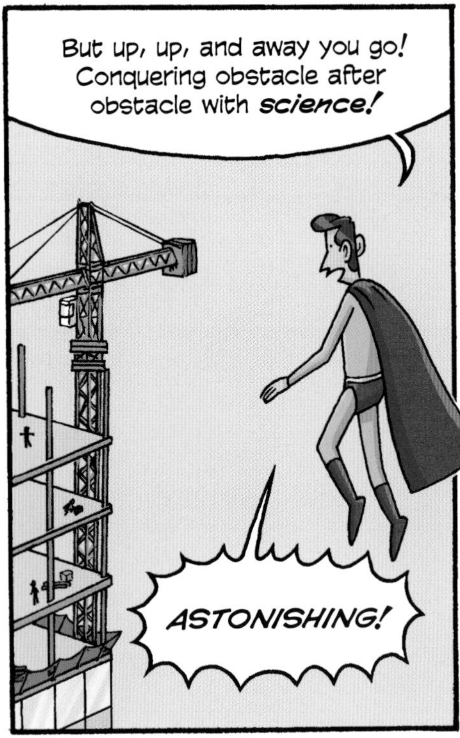
But up, up, and away you go! Conquering obstacle after obstacle with *science!*
ASTONISHING!

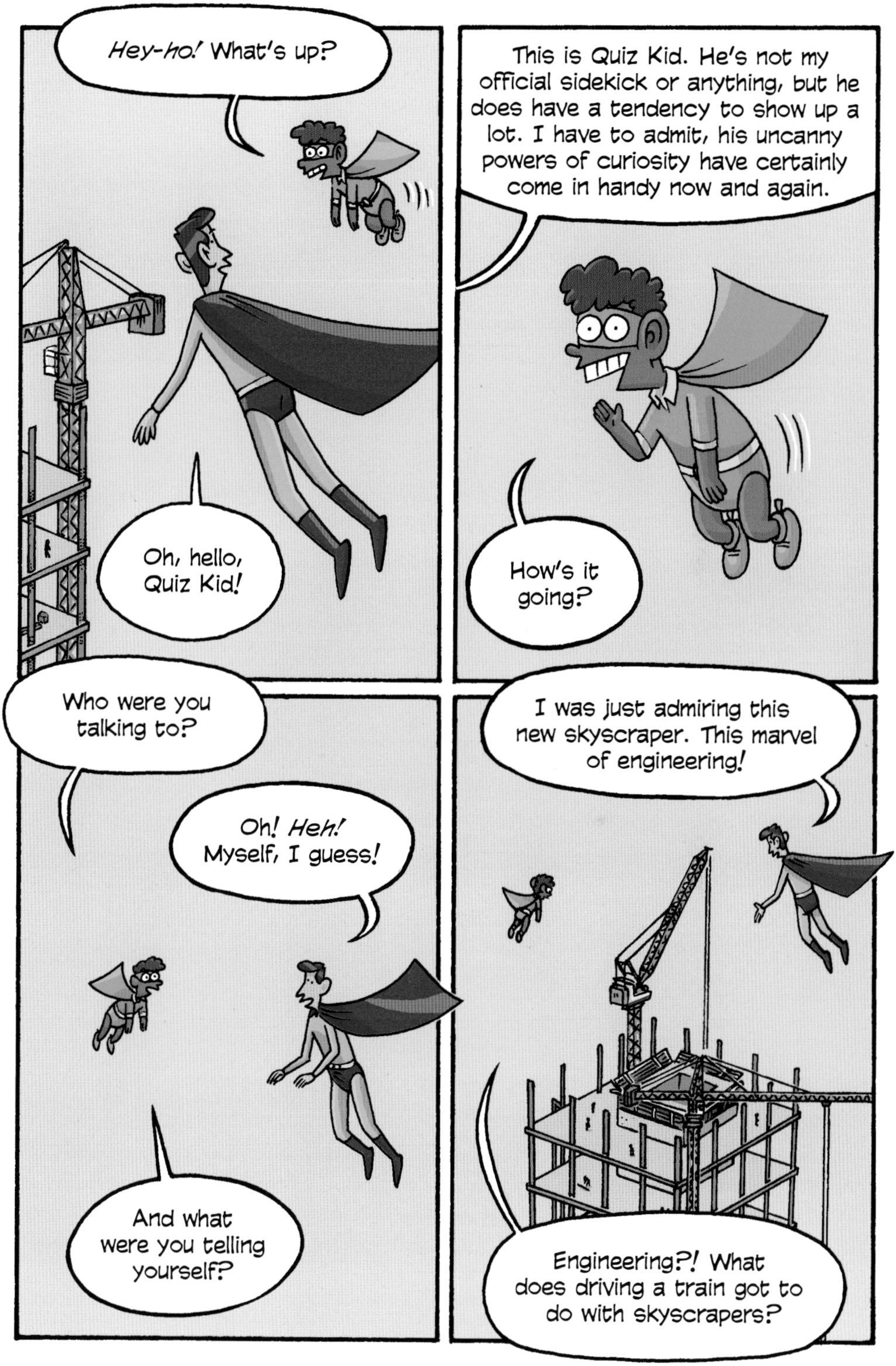
Hey-ho! What's up?
Oh, hello, Quiz Kid!
This is Quiz Kid. He's not my official sidekick or anything, but he does have a tendency to show up a lot. I have to admit, his uncanny powers of curiosity have certainly come in handy now and again.
How's it going?
Who were you talking to?
Oh! Heh! Myself, I guess!
And what were you telling yourself?
I was just admiring this new skyscraper. This marvel of engineering!
Engineering?! What does driving a train got to do with skyscrapers?

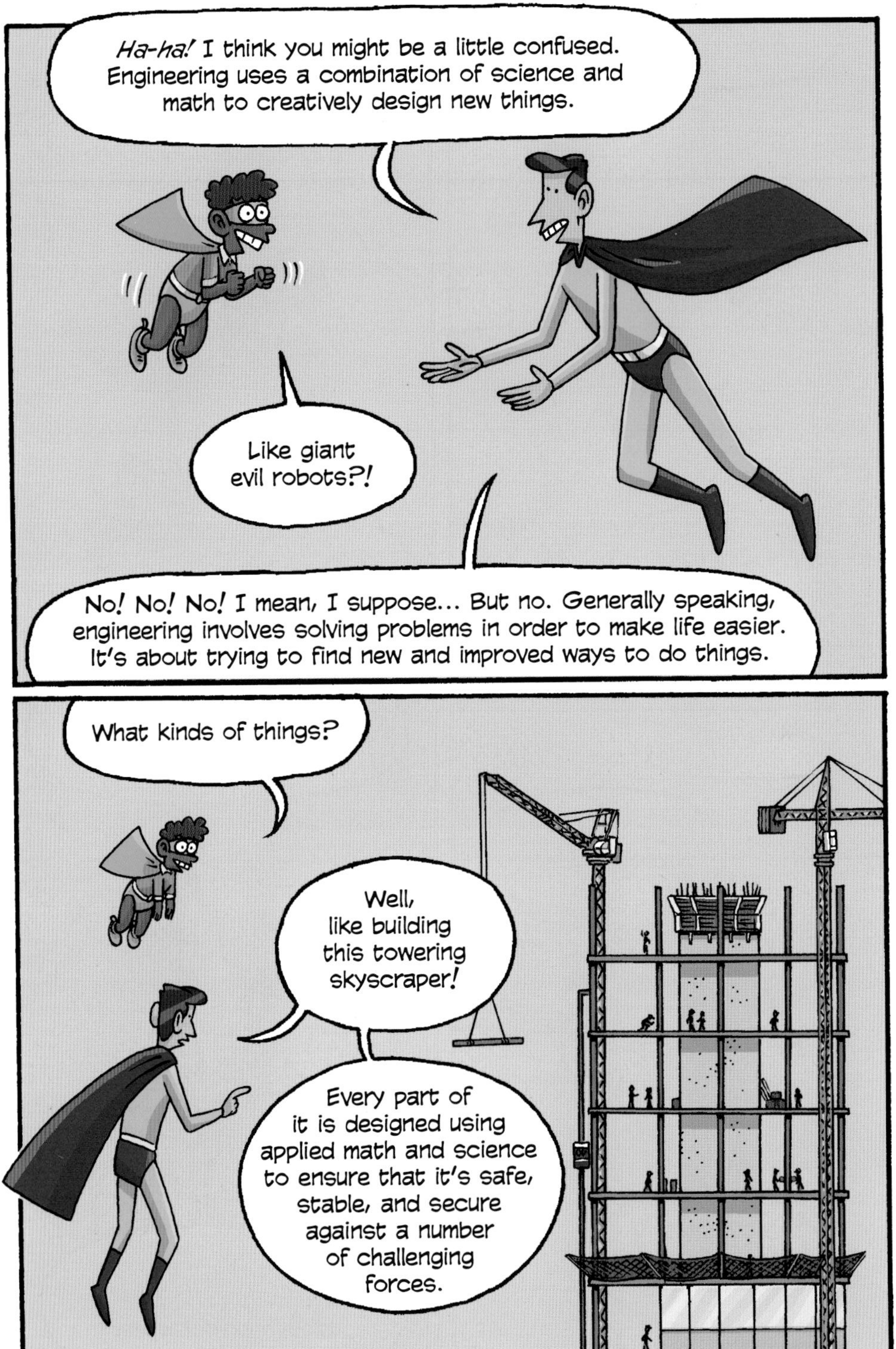

Ha-ha! I think you might be a little confused. Engineering uses a combination of science and math to creatively design new things.
Like giant evil robots?!
No! No! No! I mean, I suppose... But no. Generally speaking, engineering involves solving problems in order to make life easier. It's about trying to find new and improved ways to do things.
What kinds of things?
Well, like building this towering skyscraper!
Every part of it is designed using applied math and science to ensure that it's safe, stable, and secure against a number of challenging forces.

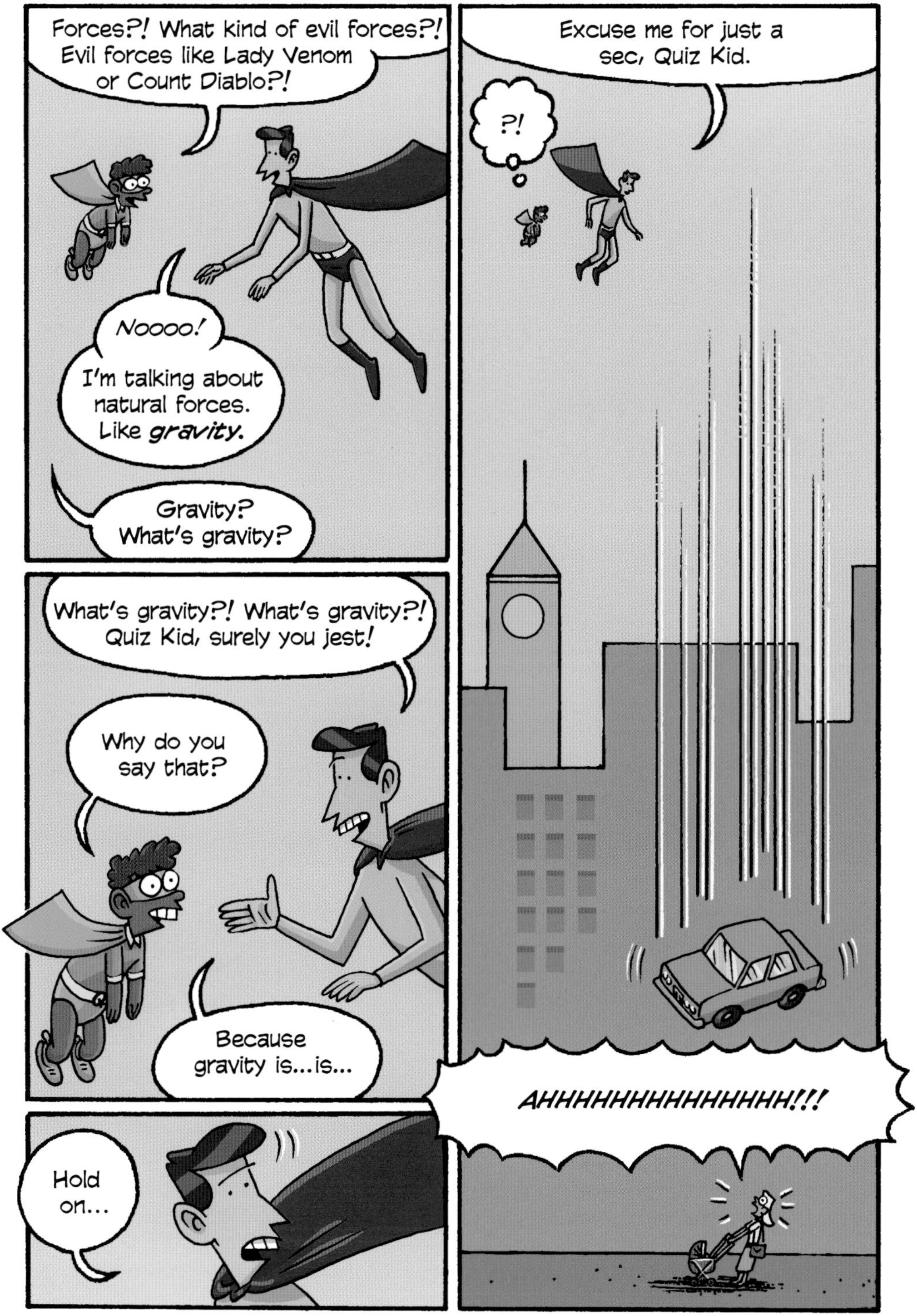
Forces?! What kind of evil forces?! Evil forces like Lady Venom or Count Diablo?!
Noooo!
I'm talking about natural forces. Like gravity.
Gravity? What's gravity?
What's gravity?! What's gravity?! Quiz Kid, surely you jest!
Why do you say that?
Because gravity is...is...
Hold on...
Excuse me for just a sec, Quiz Kid.
?!
AHHHHHHHHHHHHHH!!!

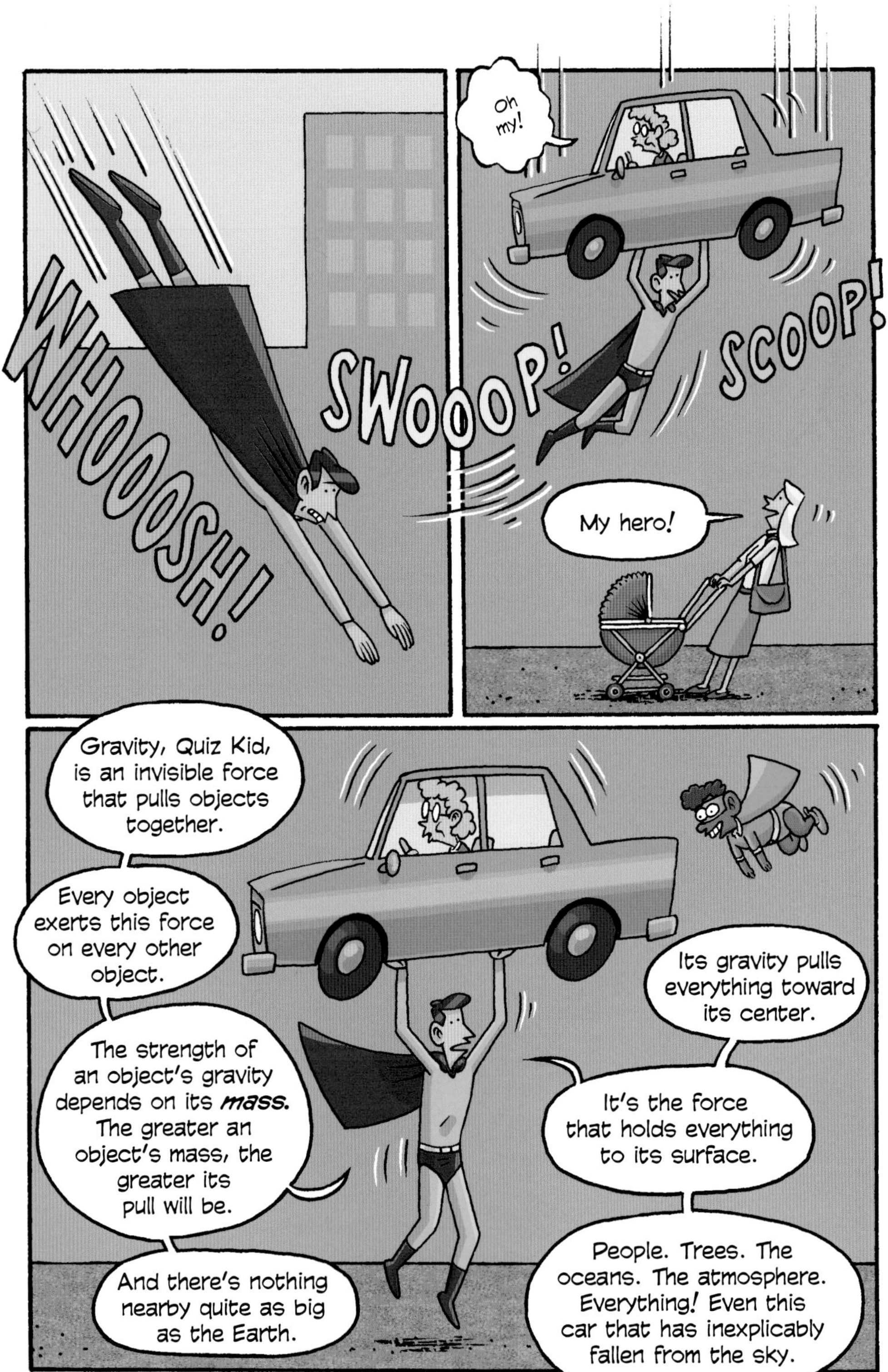
WHOOOSH!
Oh my!
SWOOOP!
SCOOP!
My hero!
Gravity, Quiz Kid, is an invisible force that pulls objects together.
Every object exerts this force on every other object.
The strength of an object's gravity depends on its ***mass.*** The greater an object's mass, the greater its pull will be.
And there's nothing nearby quite as big as the Earth.
Its gravity pulls everything toward its center.
It's the force that holds everything to its surface.
People. Trees. The oceans. The atmosphere. Everything! Even this car that has inexplicably fallen from the sky.

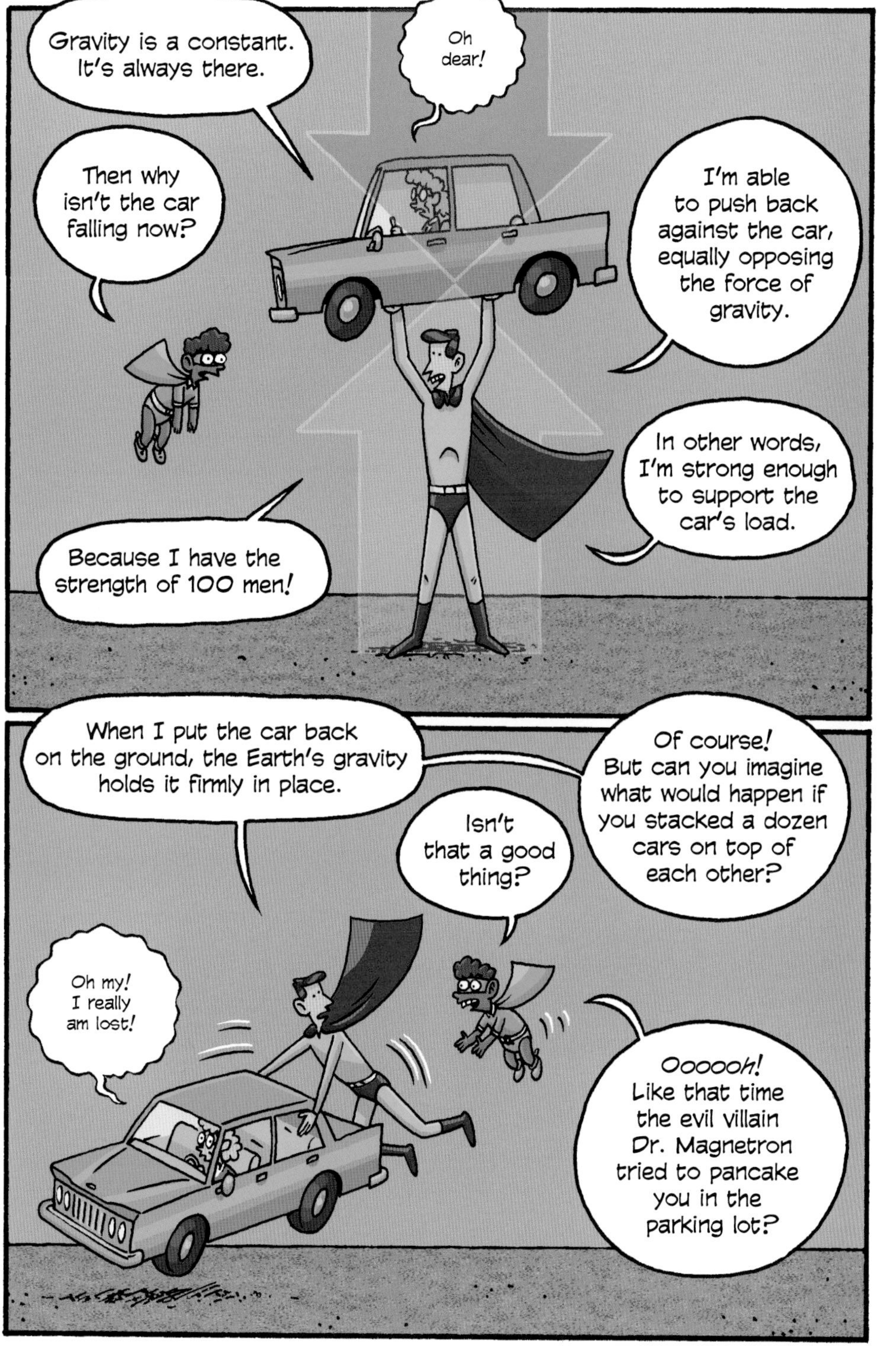
Gravity is a constant. It's always there.
Oh dear!
Then why isn't the car falling now?
I'm able to push back against the car, equally opposing the force of gravity.
In other words, I'm strong enough to support the car's load.
Because I have the strength of 100 men!
When I put the car back on the ground, the Earth's gravity holds it firmly in place.
Isn't that a good thing?
Of course! But can you imagine what would happen if you stacked a dozen cars on top of each other?
Oh my! I really am lost!
Oooooh! Like that time the evil villain Dr. Magnetron tried to pancake you in the parking lot?

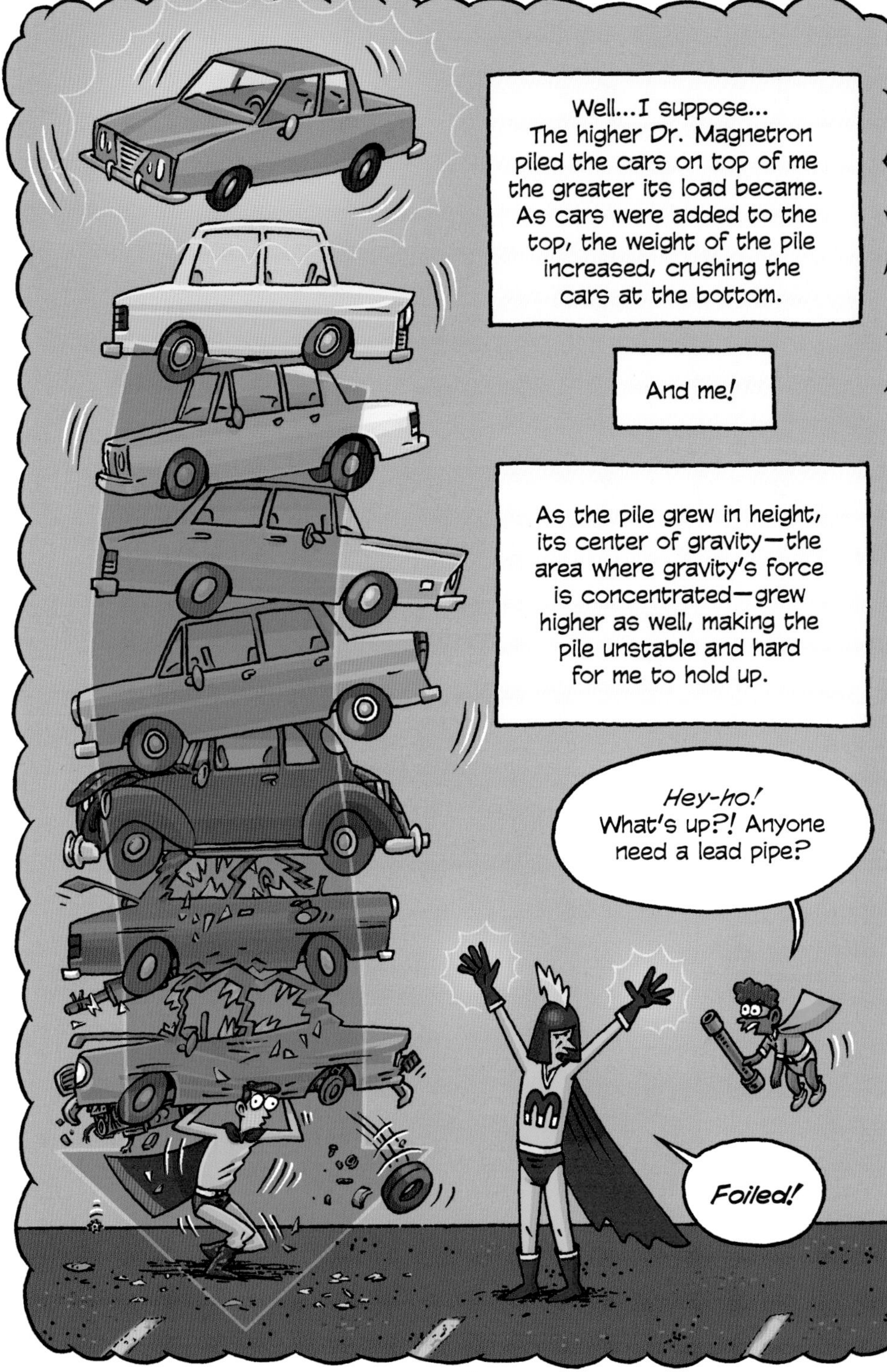
Well...I suppose... The higher Dr. Magnetron piled the cars on top of me the greater its load became. As cars were added to the top, the weight of the pile increased, crushing the cars at the bottom.
And me!
As the pile grew in height, its center of gravity—the area where gravity's force is concentrated—grew higher as well, making the pile unstable and hard for me to hold up.
Hey-ho! What's up?! Anyone need a lead pipe?
Foiled!

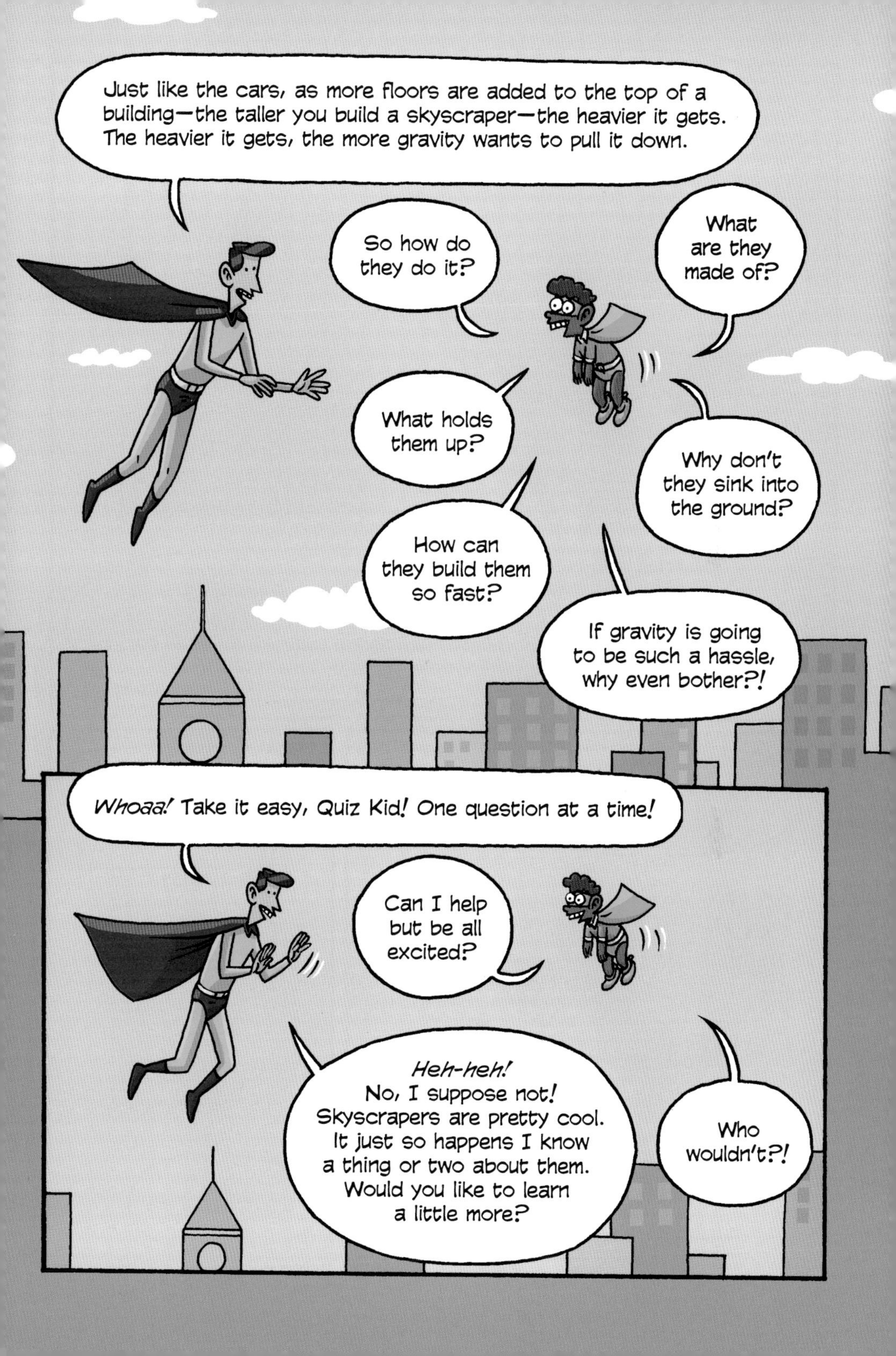
Just like the cars, as more floors are added to the top of a building—the taller you build a skyscraper—the heavier it gets. The heavier it gets, the more gravity wants to pull it down.
So how do they do it?
What are they made of?
What holds them up?
Why don't they sink into the ground?
How can they build them so fast?
If gravity is going to be such a hassle, why even bother?!
Whoaa! Take it easy, Quiz Kid! One question at a time!
Can I help but be all excited?
Heh-heh! No, I suppose not! Skyscrapers are pretty cool. It just so happens I know a thing or two about them. Would you like to learn a little more?
Who wouldn't?!

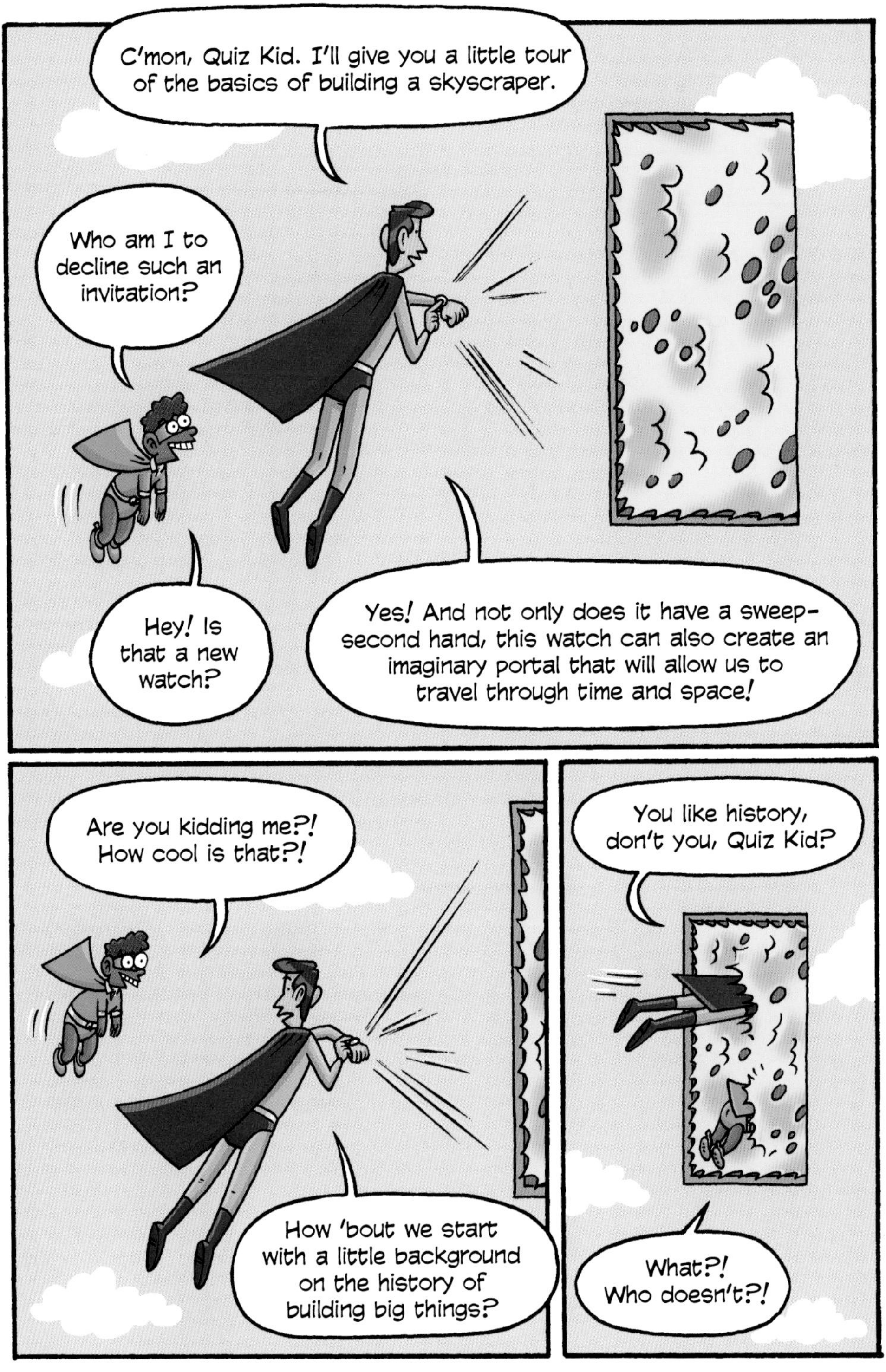
C'mon, Quiz Kid. I'll give you a little tour of the basics of building a skyscraper.
Who am I to decline such an invitation?
Hey! Is that a new watch?
Yes! And not only does it have a sweep-second hand, this watch can also create an imaginary portal that will allow us to travel through time and space!
Are you kidding me?! How cool is that?!
How 'bout we start with a little background on the history of building big things?
You like history, don't you, Quiz Kid?
What?! Who doesn't?!

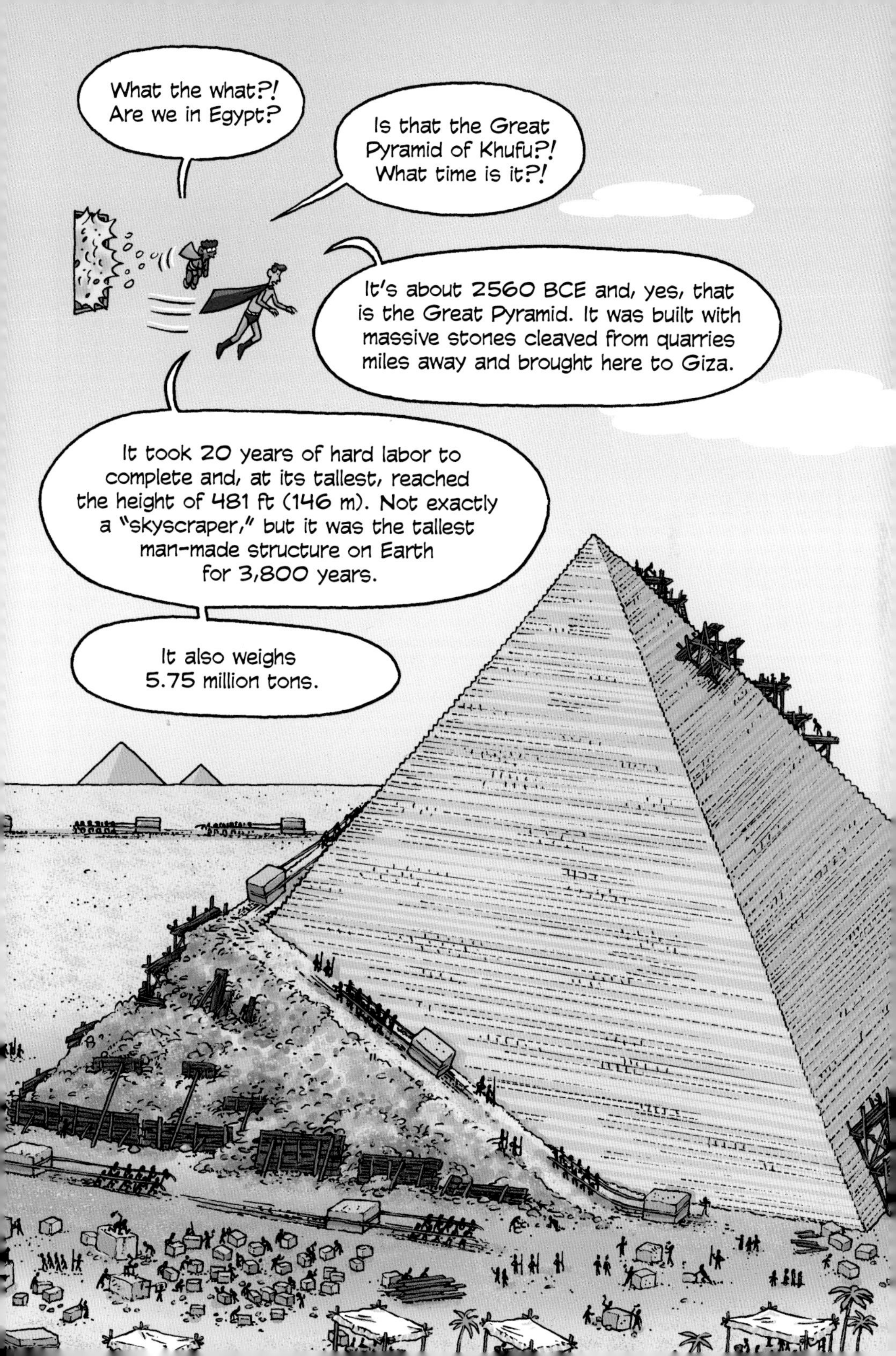
What the what?! Are we in Egypt?
Is that the Great Pyramid of Khufu?! What time is it?!
It's about 2560 BCE and, yes, that is the Great Pyramid. It was built with massive stones cleaved from quarries miles away and brought here to Giza.
It took 20 years of hard labor to complete and, at its tallest, reached the height of 481 ft (146 m). Not exactly a "skyscraper," but it was the tallest man-made structure on Earth for 3,800 years.
It also weighs 5.75 million tons.

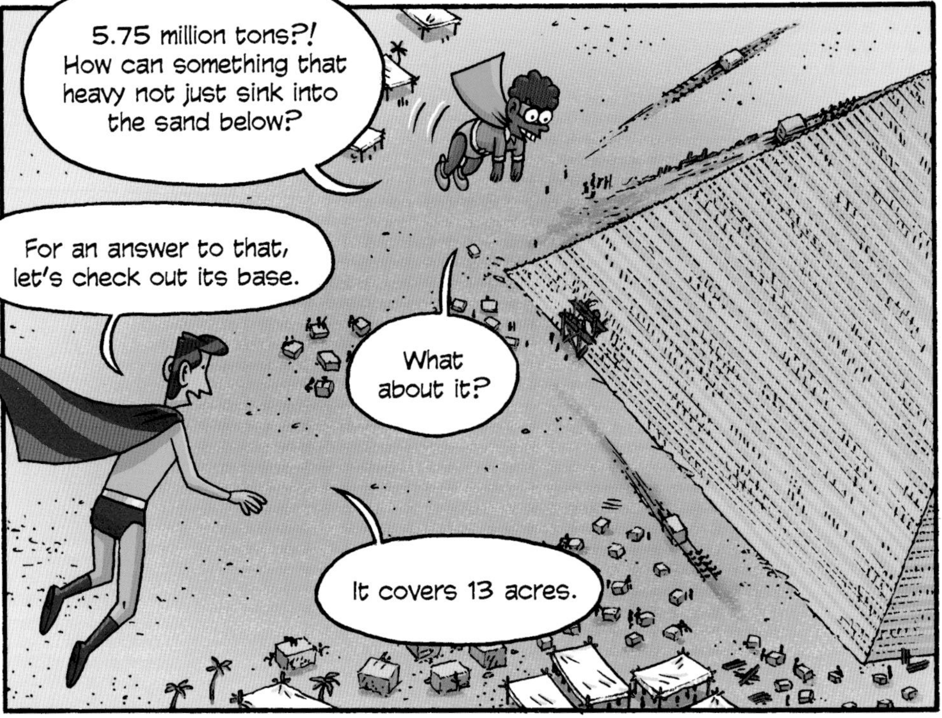
5.75 million tons?! How can something that heavy not just sink into the sand below?
For an answer to that, let's check out its base.
What about it?
It covers 13 acres.

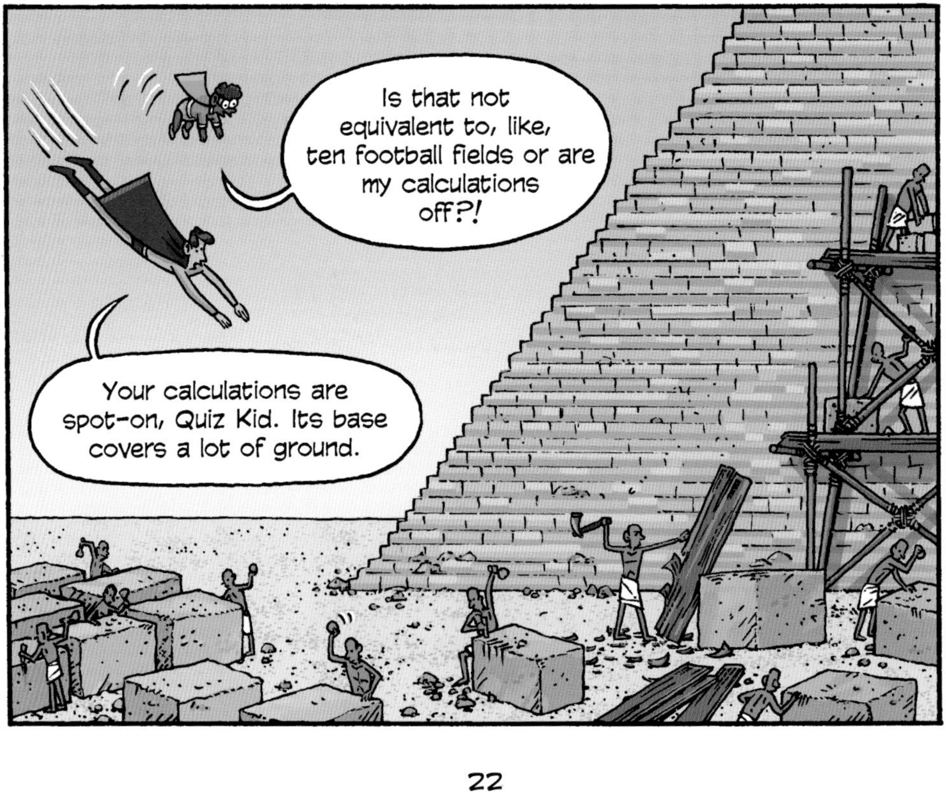
Is that not equivalent to, like, ten football fields or are my calculations off?!
Your calculations are spot-on, Quiz Kid. Its base covers a lot of ground.

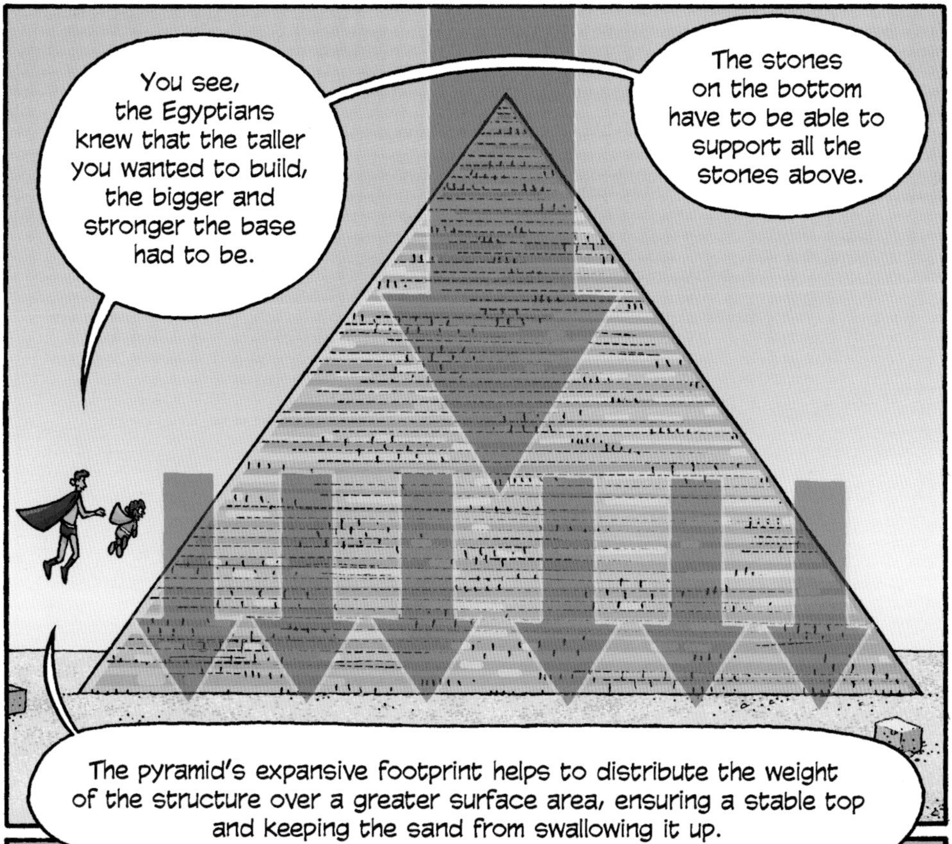
You see, the Egyptians knew that the taller you wanted to build, the bigger and stronger the base had to be.
The stones on the bottom have to be able to support all the stones above.
The pyramid's expansive footprint helps to distribute the weight of the structure over a greater surface area, ensuring a stable top and keeping the sand from swallowing it up.

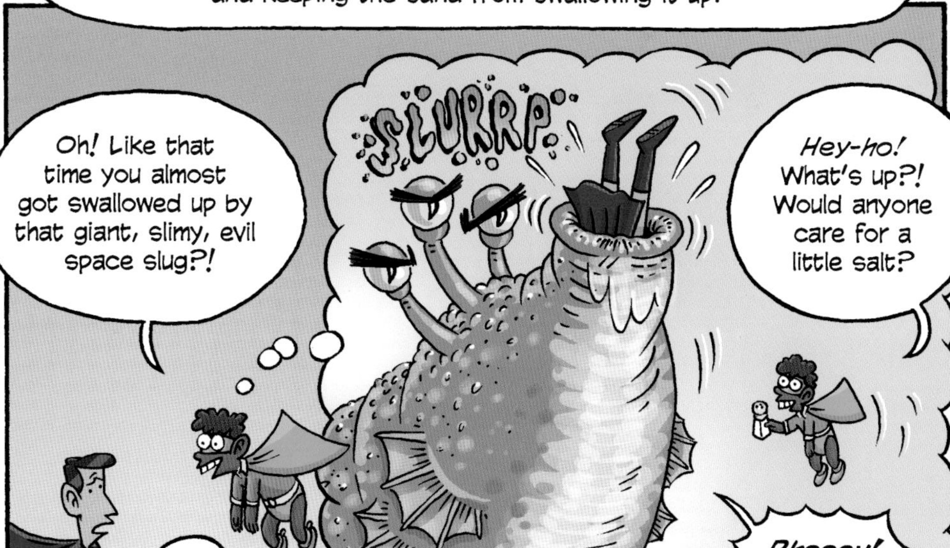
Oh! Like that time you almost got swallowed up by that giant, slimy, evil space slug?!
SLURRP
Hey-ho! What's up?! Would anyone care for a little salt?
Uh...
Phooey!

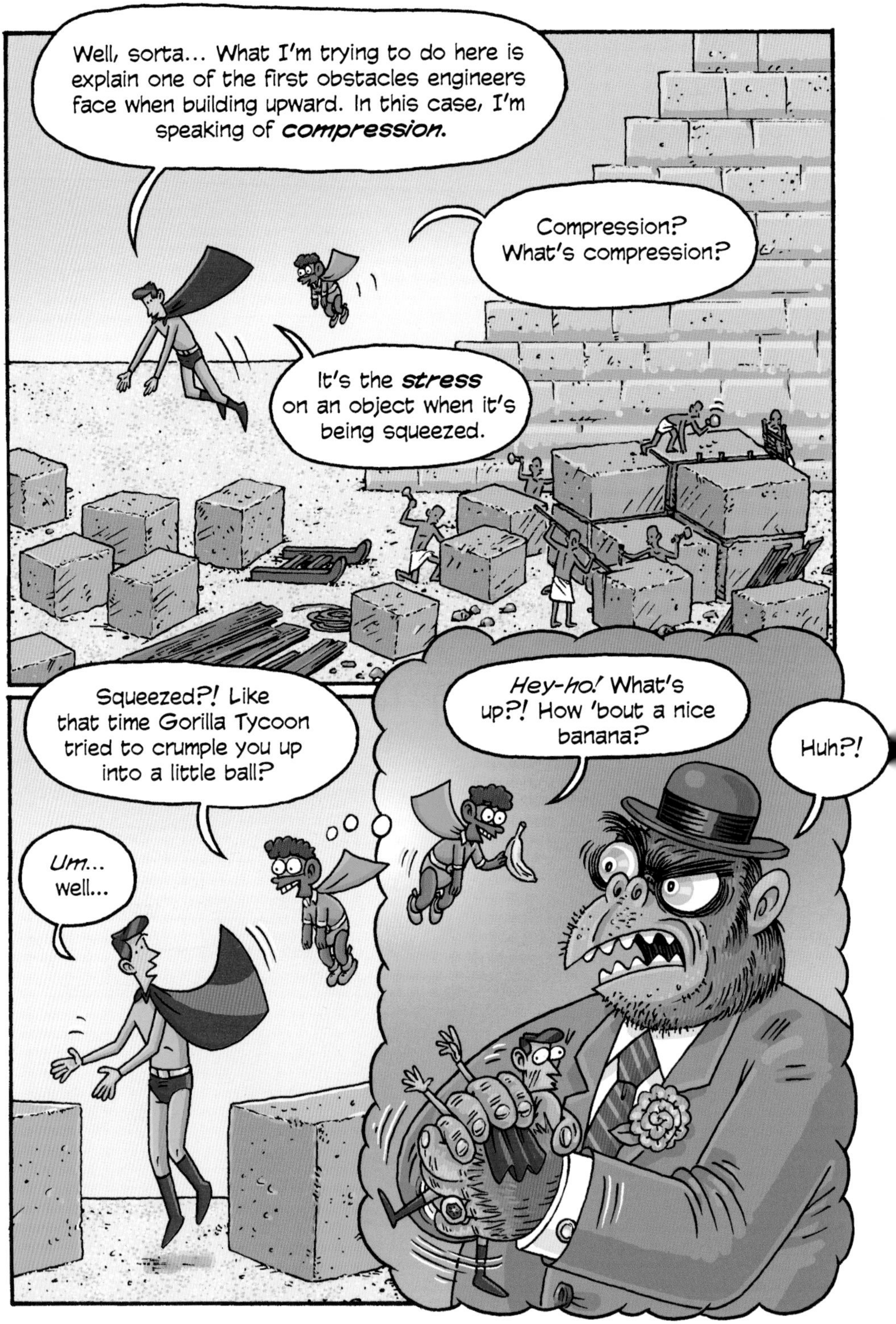

Well, sorta... What I'm trying to do here is explain one of the first obstacles engineers face when building upward. In this case, I'm speaking of ***compression.***
Compression? What's compression?
It's the ***stress*** on an object when it's being squeezed.
Squeezed?! Like that time Gorilla Tycoon tried to crumple you up into a little ball?
Um... well...
Hey-ho! What's up?! How 'bout a nice banana?
Huh?!

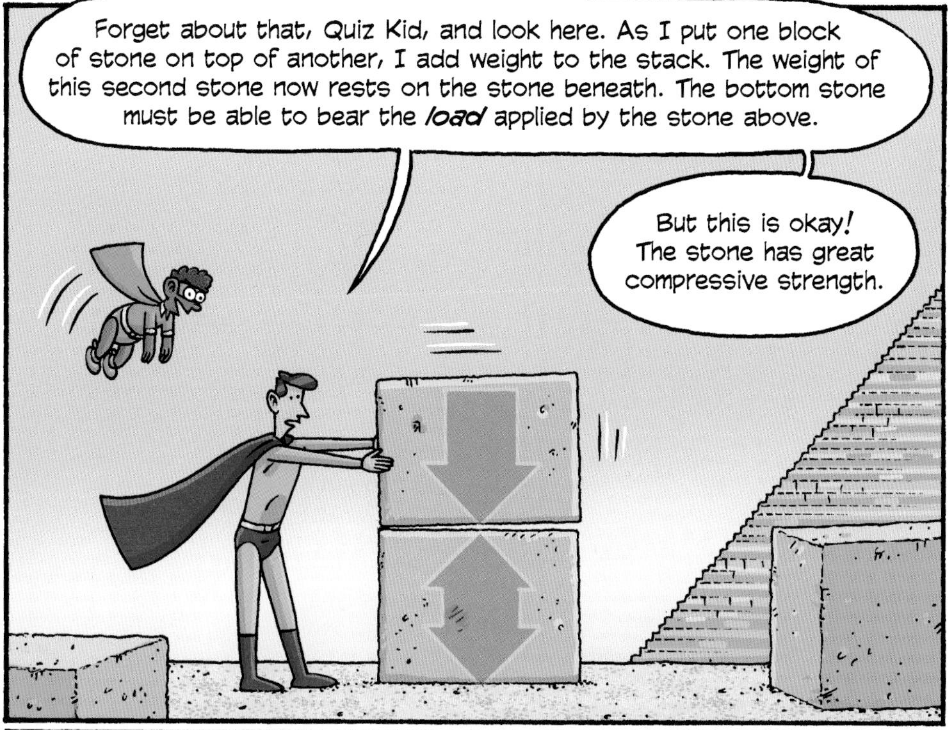
Forget about that, Quiz Kid, and look here. As I put one block of stone on top of another, I add weight to the stack. The weight of this second stone now rests on the stone beneath. The bottom stone must be able to bear the *load* applied by the stone above.
But this is okay! The stone has great compressive strength.

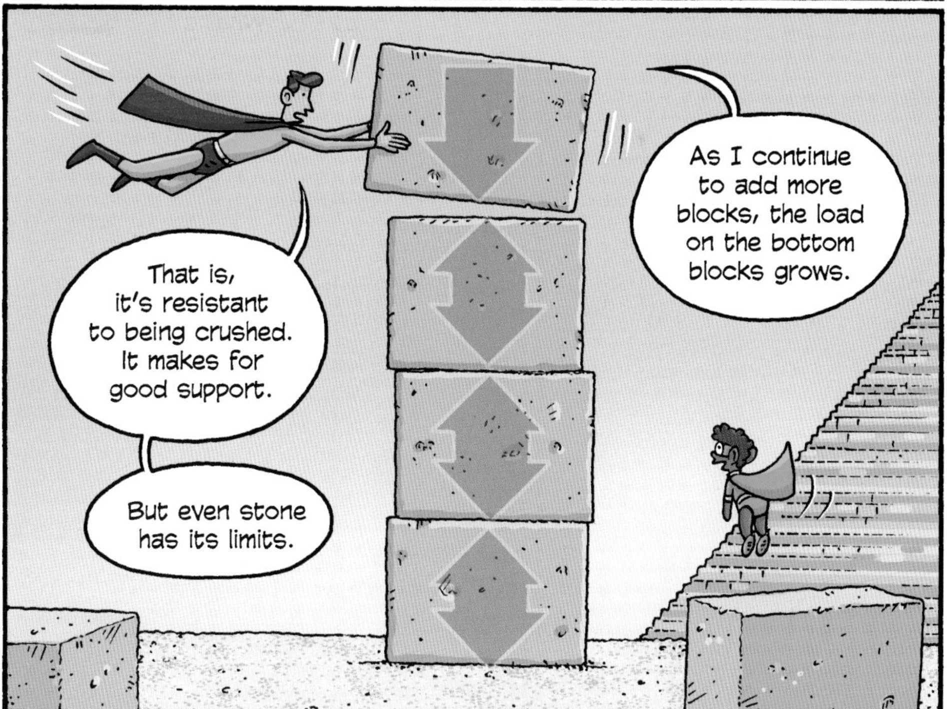
That is, it's resistant to being crushed. It makes for good support.
But even stone has its limits.
As I continue to add more blocks, the load on the bottom blocks grows.

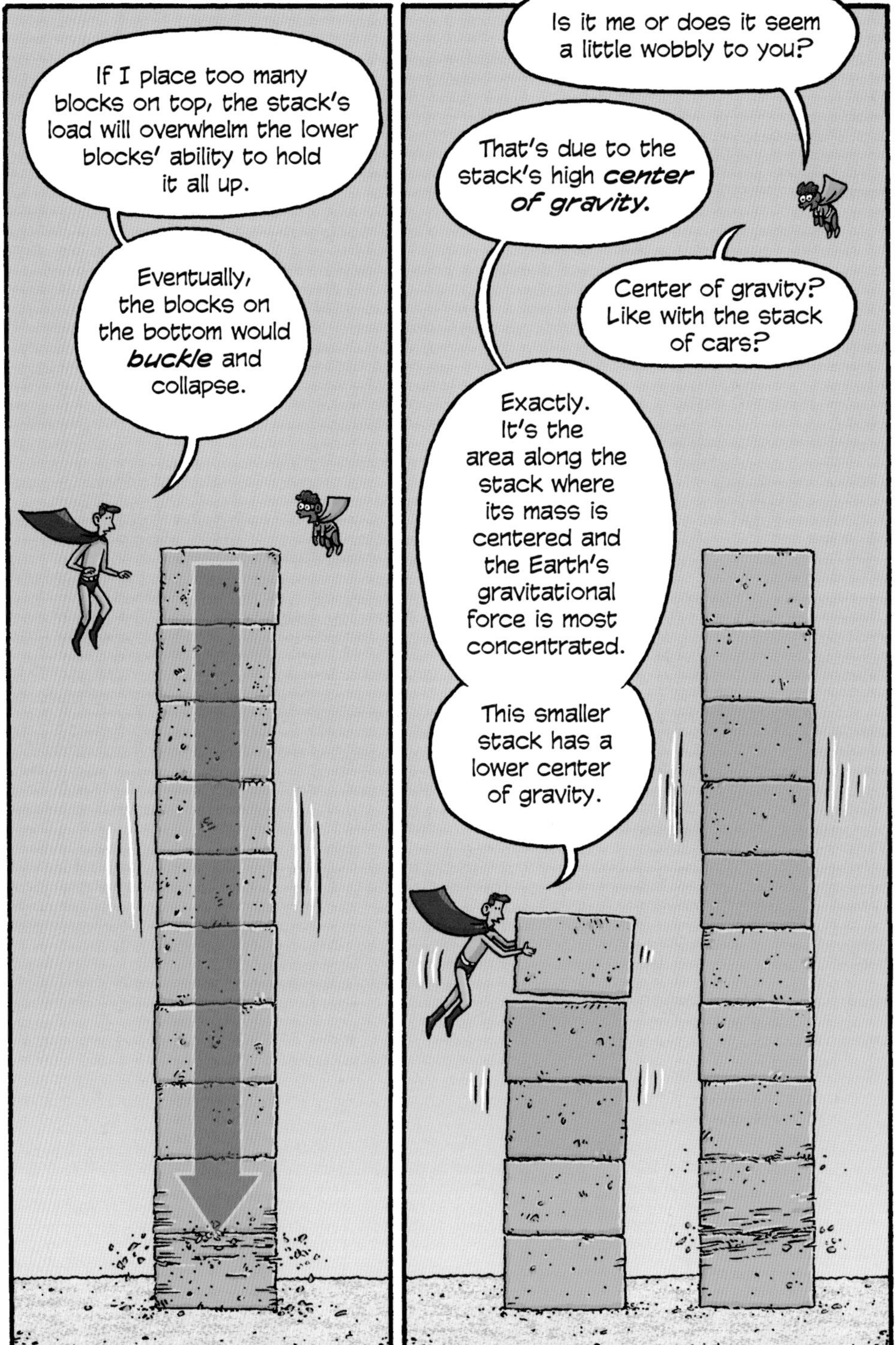
If I place too many blocks on top, the stack's load will overwhelm the lower blocks' ability to hold it all up.
Eventually, the blocks on the bottom would *buckle* and collapse.
Is it me or does it seem a little wobbly to you?
That's due to the stack's high *center of gravity.*
Center of gravity? Like with the stack of cars?
Exactly. It's the area along the stack where its mass is centered and the Earth's gravitational force is most concentrated.
This smaller stack has a lower center of gravity.

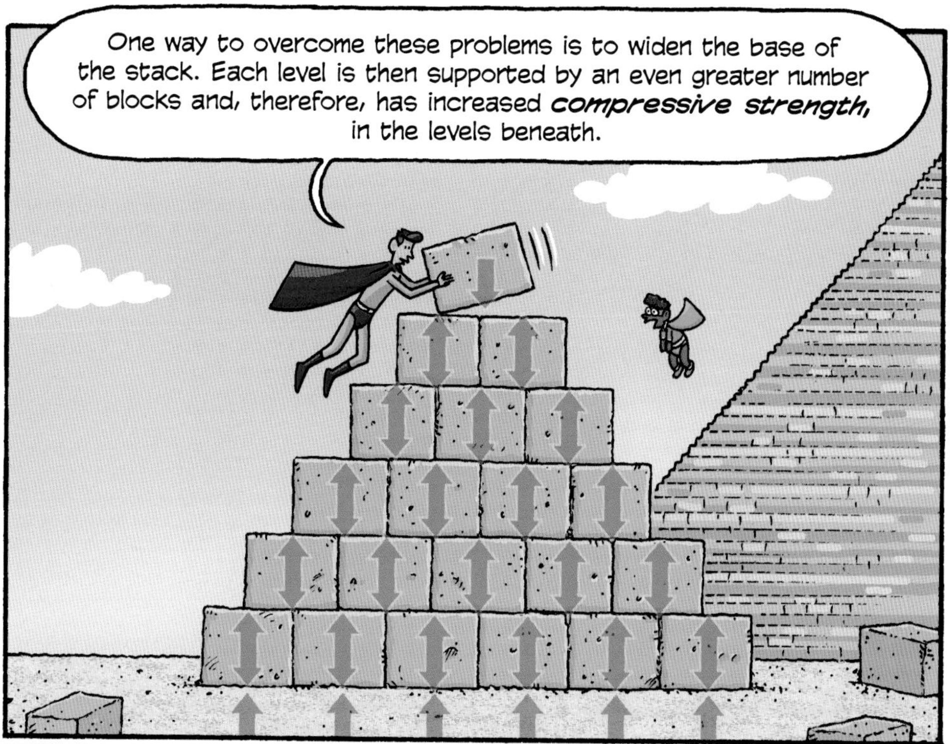
One way to overcome these problems is to widen the base of the stack. Each level is then supported by an even greater number of blocks and, therefore, has increased ***compressive strength,*** in the levels beneath.

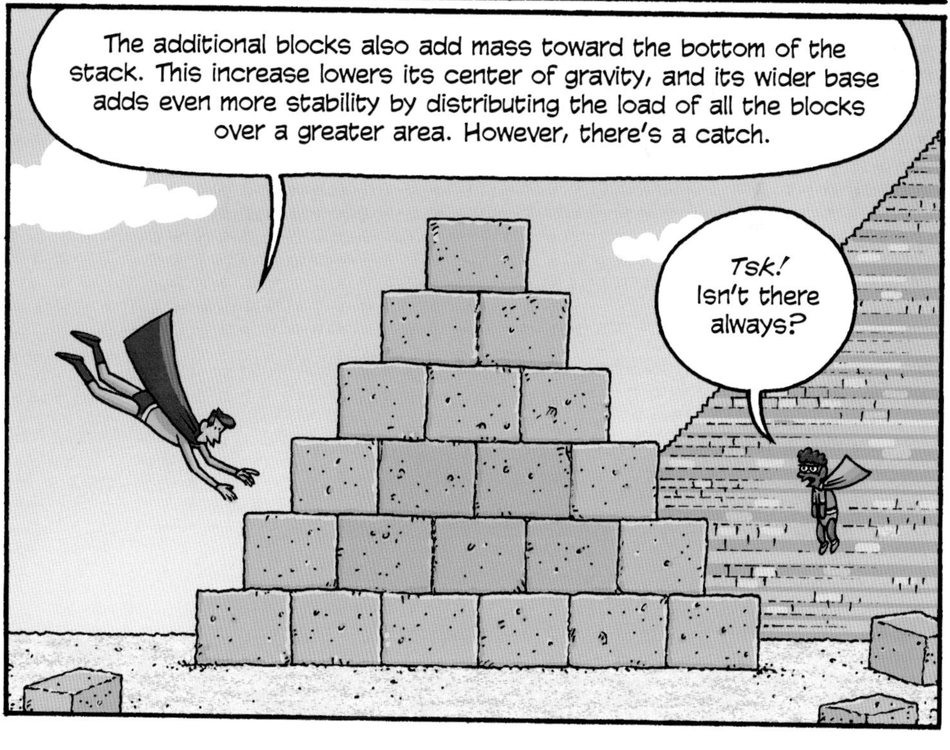
The additional blocks also add mass toward the bottom of the stack. This increase lowers its center of gravity, and its wider base adds even more stability by distributing the load of all the blocks over a greater area. However, there's a catch.
Tsk! Isn't there always?

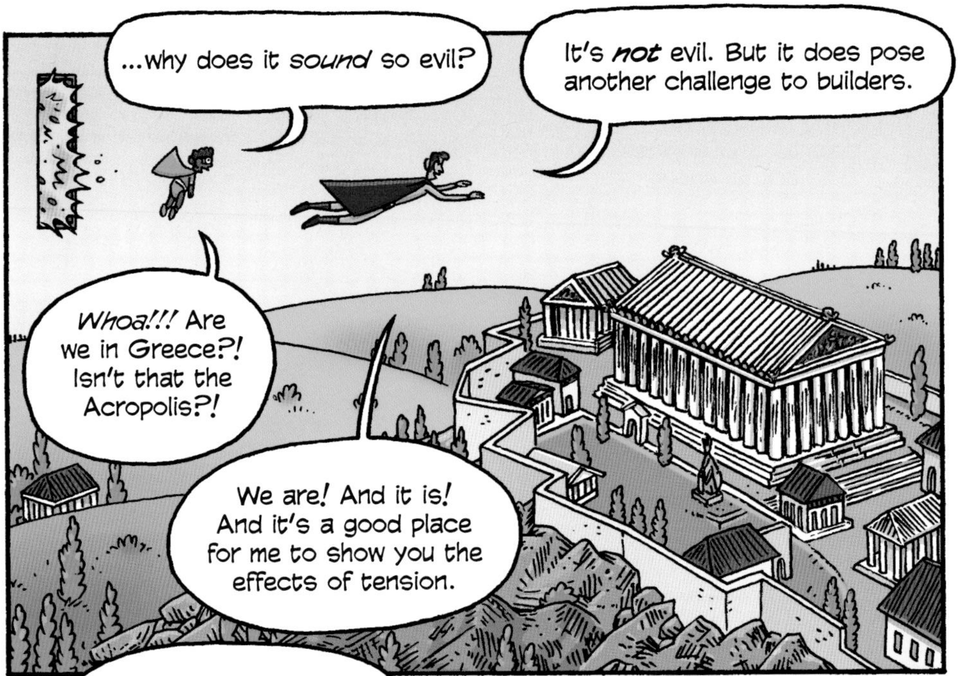
...why does it *sound* so evil?
It's **not** evil. But it does pose another challenge to builders.
Whoa!!! Are we in Greece?! Isn't that the Acropolis?!
We are! And it is! And it's a good place for me to show you the effects of tension.

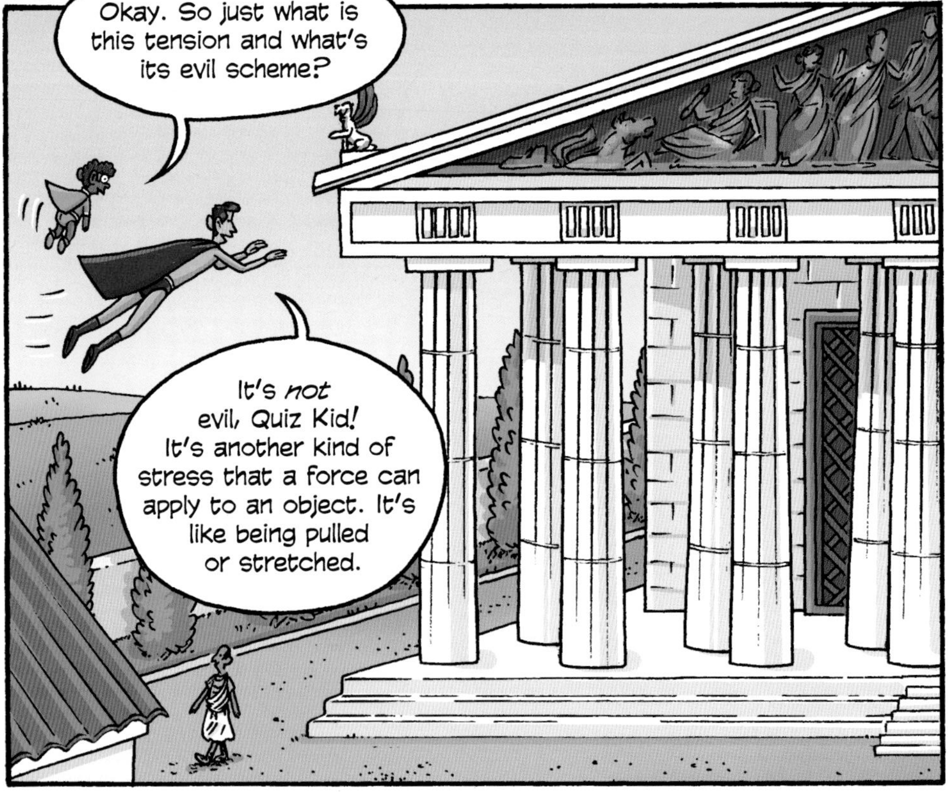
Okay. So just what is this tension and what's its evil scheme?
It's *not* evil, Quiz Kid! It's another kind of stress that a force can apply to an object. It's like being pulled or stretched.

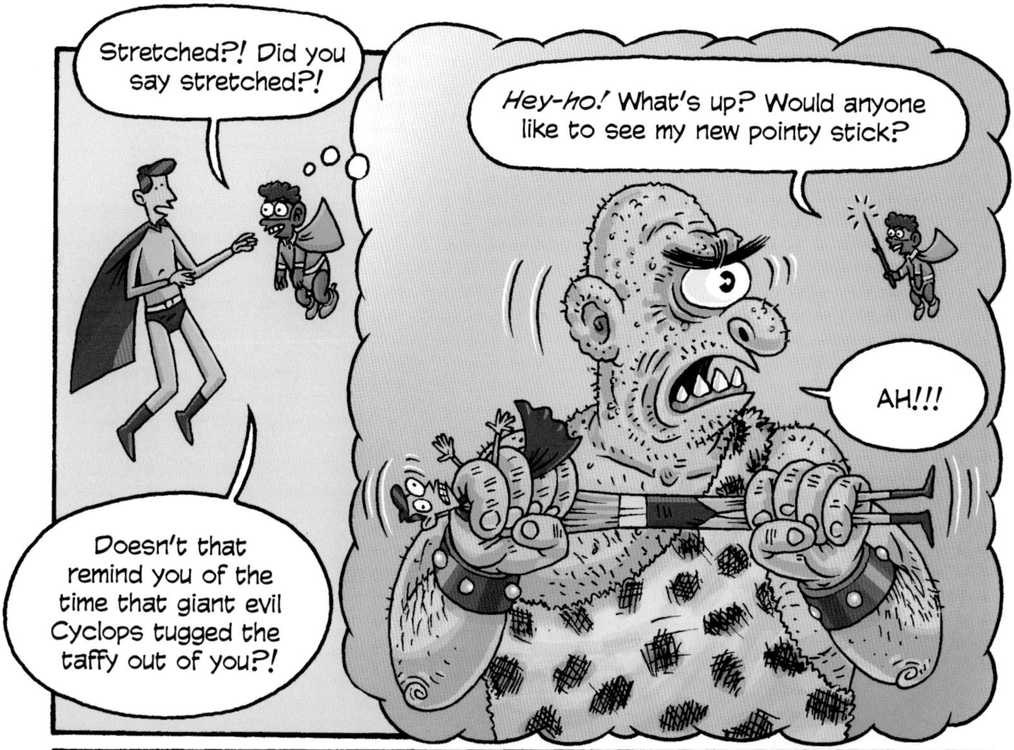
Stretched?! Did you say stretched?!
Hey-ho! What's up? Would anyone like to see my new pointy stick?
AH!!!
Doesn't that remind you of the time that giant evil Cyclops tugged the taffy out of you?!

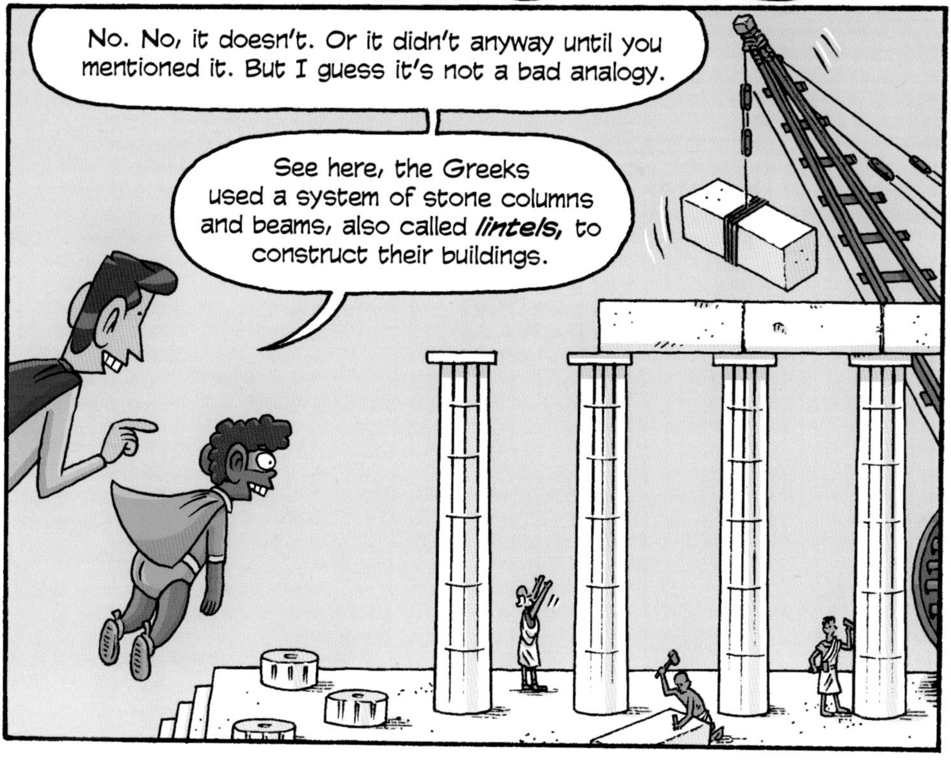
No. No, it doesn't. Or it didn't anyway until you mentioned it. But I guess it's not a bad analogy.
See here, the Greeks used a system of stone columns and beams, also called *lintels,* to construct their buildings.

33

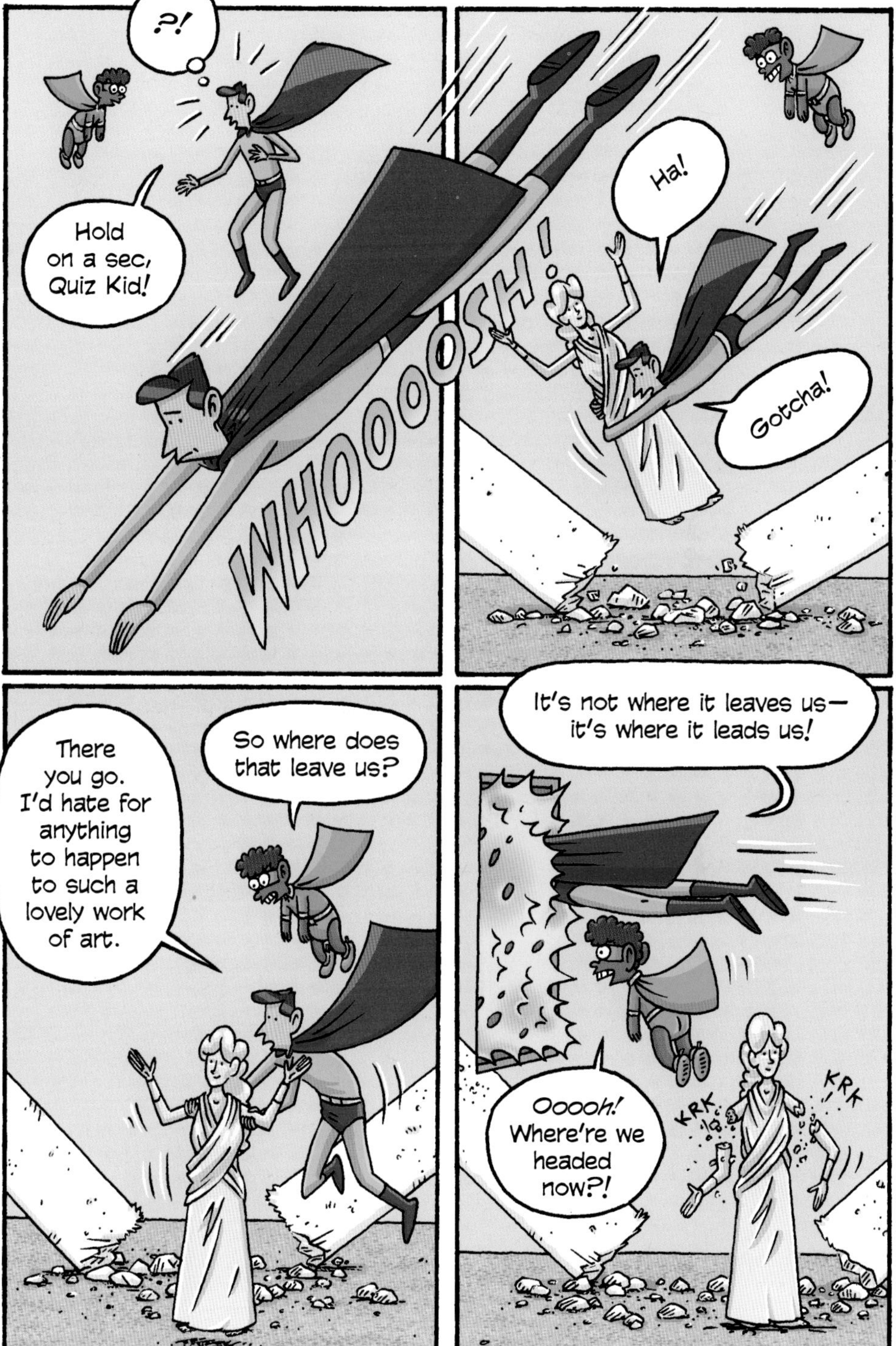
?!
Hold on a sec, Quiz Kid!
WHOOOOSH!
Ha!
Gotcha!
There you go. I'd hate for anything to happen to such a lovely work of art.
So where does that leave us?
It's not where it leaves us—it's where it leads us!
Ooooh! Where're we headed now?!
KRK
KRK

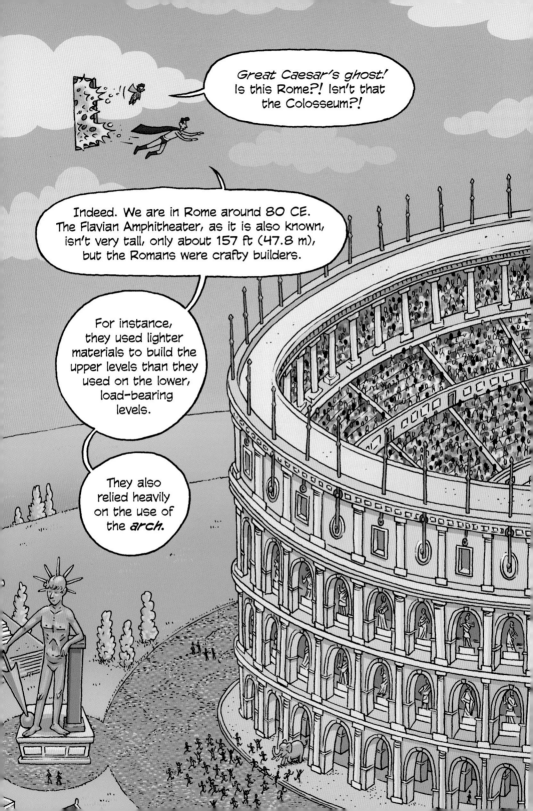

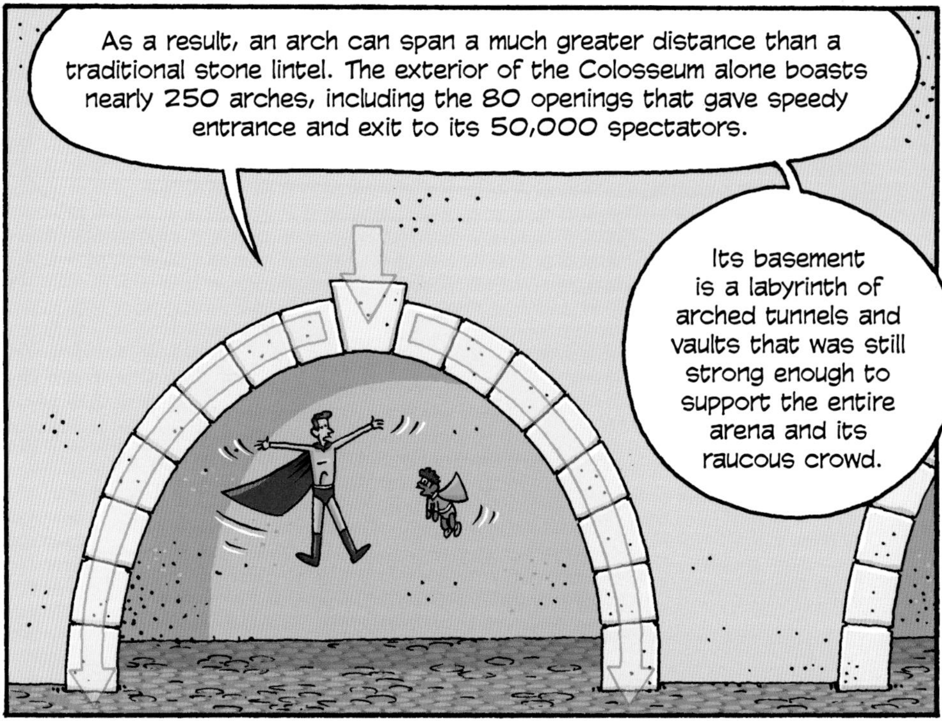
As a result, an arch can span a much greater distance than a traditional stone lintel. The exterior of the Colosseum alone boasts nearly 250 arches, including the 80 openings that gave speedy entrance and exit to its 50,000 spectators.
Its basement is a labyrinth of arched tunnels and vaults that was still strong enough to support the entire arena and its raucous crowd.

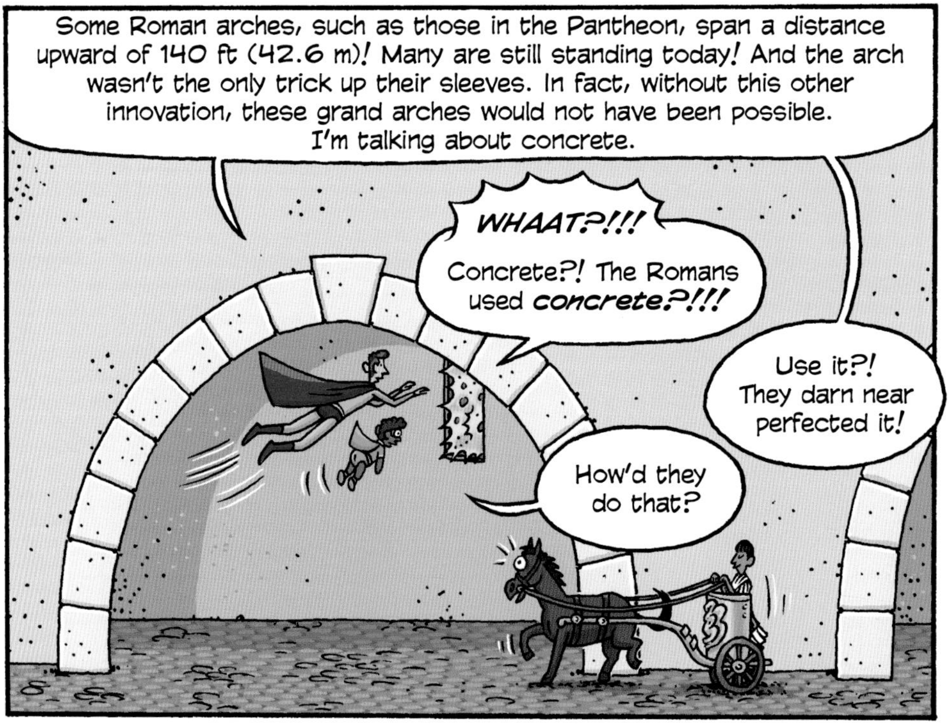
Some Roman arches, such as those in the Pantheon, span a distance upward of 140 ft (42.6 m)! Many are still standing today! And the arch wasn't the only trick up their sleeves. In fact, without this other innovation, these grand arches would not have been possible. I'm talking about concrete.
WHAAT?!!! Concrete?! The Romans used concrete?!!!
Use it?! They darn near perfected it!
How'd they do that?

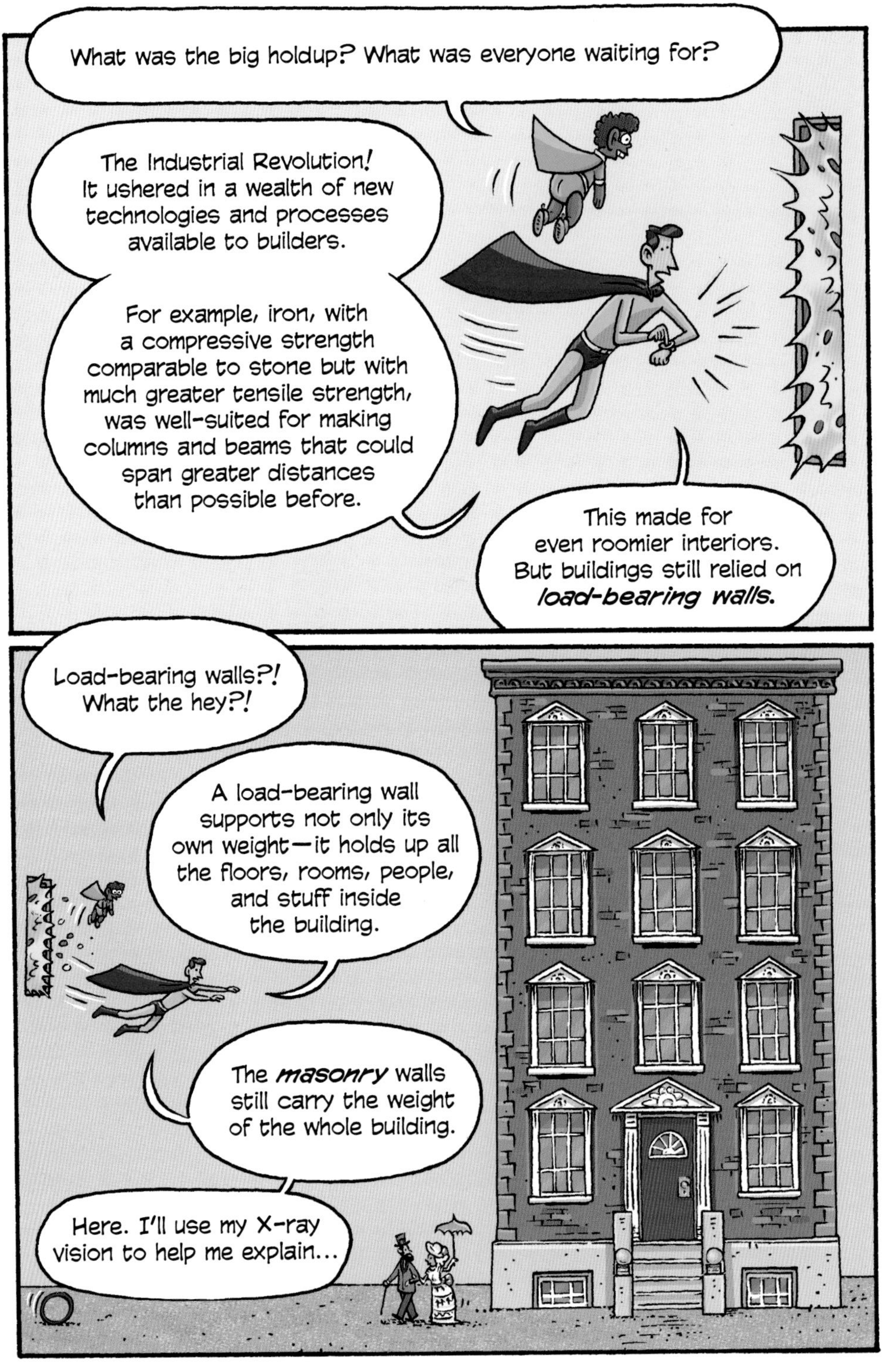
What was the big holdup? What was everyone waiting for?
The Industrial Revolution! It ushered in a wealth of new technologies and processes available to builders.
For example, iron, with a compressive strength comparable to stone but with much greater tensile strength, was well-suited for making columns and beams that could span greater distances than possible before.
This made for even roomier interiors. But buildings still relied on *load-bearing walls.*
Load-bearing walls?! What the hey?!
A load-bearing wall supports not only its own weight—it holds up all the floors, rooms, people, and stuff inside the building.
The *masonry* walls still carry the weight of the whole building.
Here. I'll use my X-ray vision to help me explain...

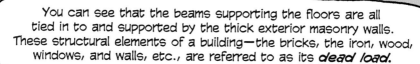

You can see that the beams supporting the floors are all tied in to and supported by the thick exterior masonry walls. These structural elements of a building—the bricks, the iron, wood, windows, and walls, etc., are referred to as its *dead load.*

The walls need to support the building's *live load,* as well.

The live load is the weight added by all the things in the building like furniture and people and pets and stuff shifting about inside.

So what happens next?

Well, in the mid-1800s a series of events and *innovations* paved the way for the first modern skyscrapers.

What kind of innovations?

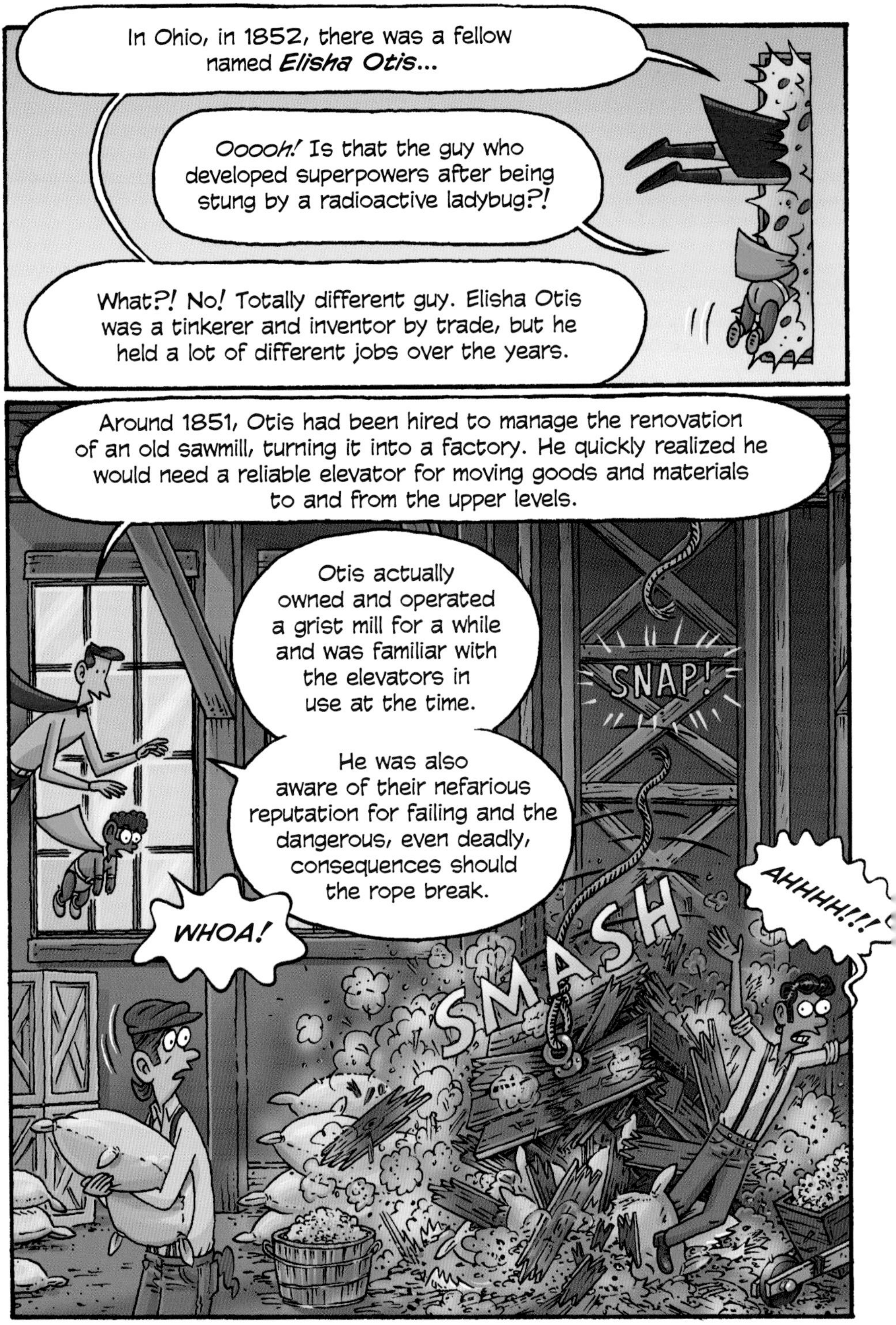
In Ohio, in 1852, there was a fellow named *Elisha Otis*...
Ooooh! Is that the guy who developed superpowers after being stung by a radioactive ladybug?!
What?! No! Totally different guy. Elisha Otis was a tinkerer and inventor by trade, but he held a lot of different jobs over the years.
Around 1851, Otis had been hired to manage the renovation of an old sawmill, turning it into a factory. He quickly realized he would need a reliable elevator for moving goods and materials to and from the upper levels.
Otis actually owned and operated a grist mill for a while and was familiar with the elevators in use at the time.
He was also aware of their nefarious reputation for failing and the dangerous, even deadly, consequences should the rope break.
SNAP!
WHOA!
SMASH
AHHHH!!!!

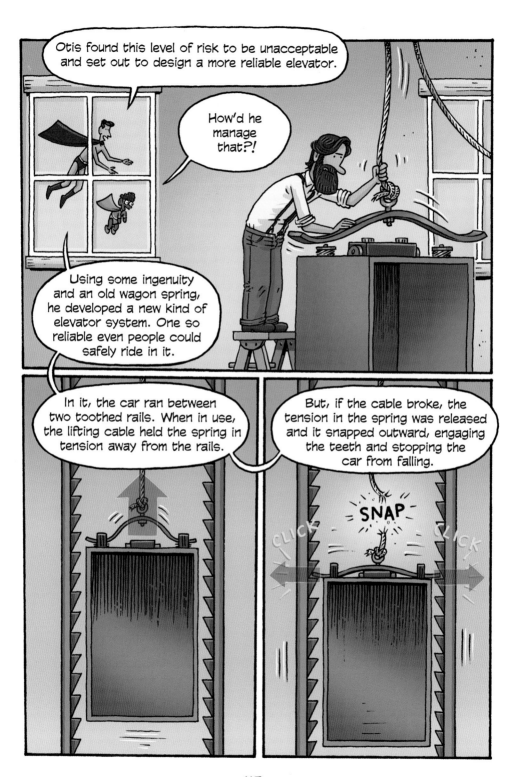

45

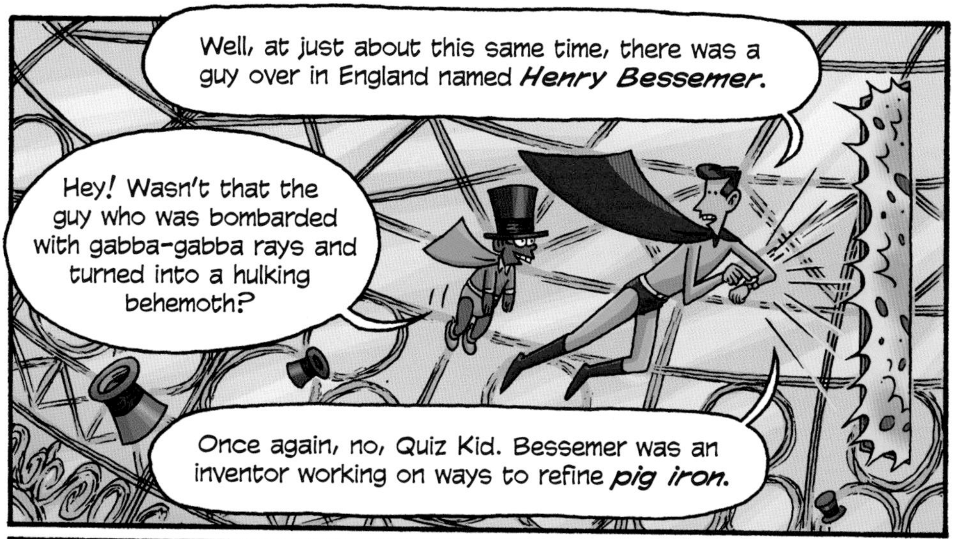
Well, at just about this same time, there was a guy over in England named *Henry Bessemer.*
Hey! Wasn't that the guy who was bombarded with gabba-gabba rays and turned into a hulking behemoth?
Once again, no, Quiz Kid. Bessemer was an inventor working on ways to refine *pig iron.*

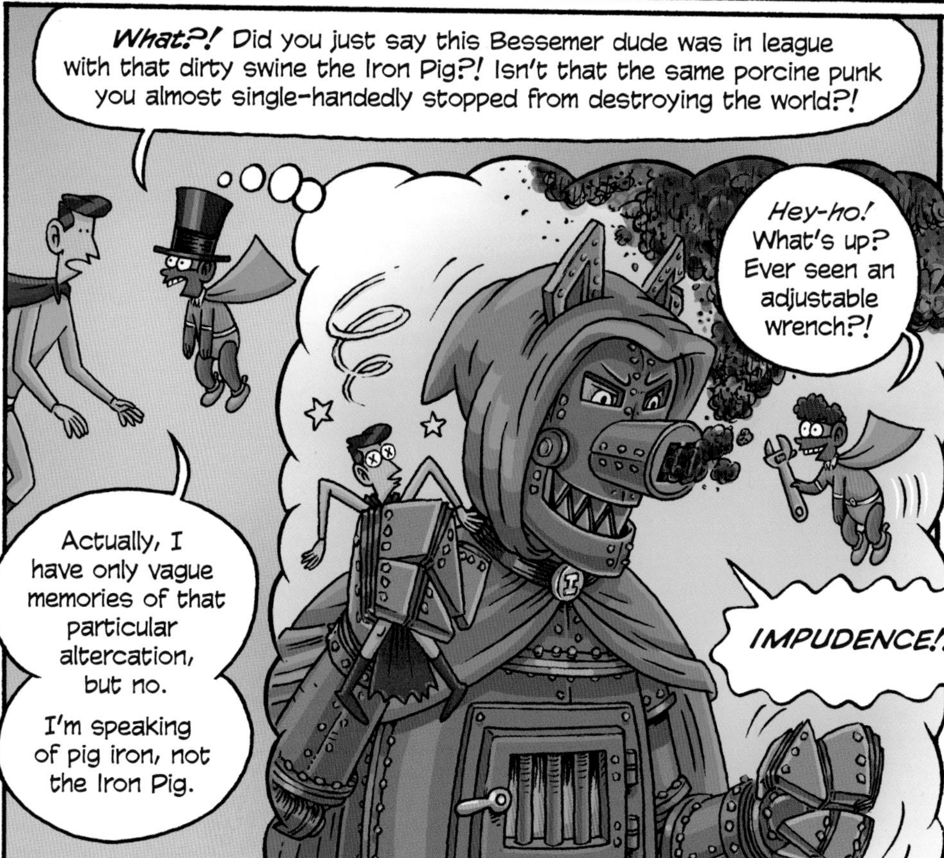
What?! Did you just say this Bessemer dude was in league with that dirty swine the Iron Pig?! Isn't that the same porcine punk you almost single-handedly stopped from destroying the world?!
Hey-ho! What's up? Ever seen an adjustable wrench?!
IMPUDENCE!!!
Actually, I have only vague memories of that particular altercation, but no.
I'm speaking of pig iron, not the Iron Pig.

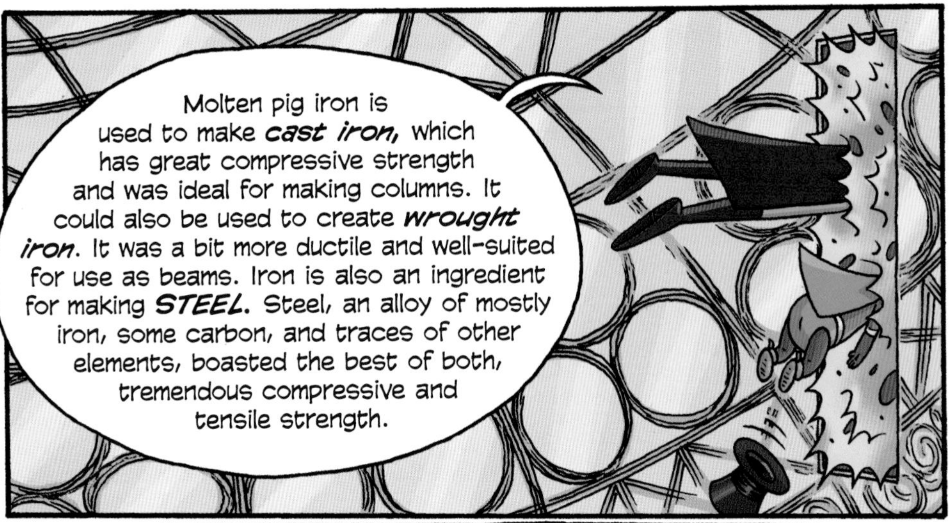
Molten pig iron is used to make *cast iron,* which has great compressive strength and was ideal for making columns. It could also be used to create *wrought iron*. It was a bit more ductile and well-suited for use as beams. Iron is also an ingredient for making **STEEL.** Steel, an alloy of mostly iron, some carbon, and traces of other elements, boasted the best of both, tremendous compressive and tensile strength.

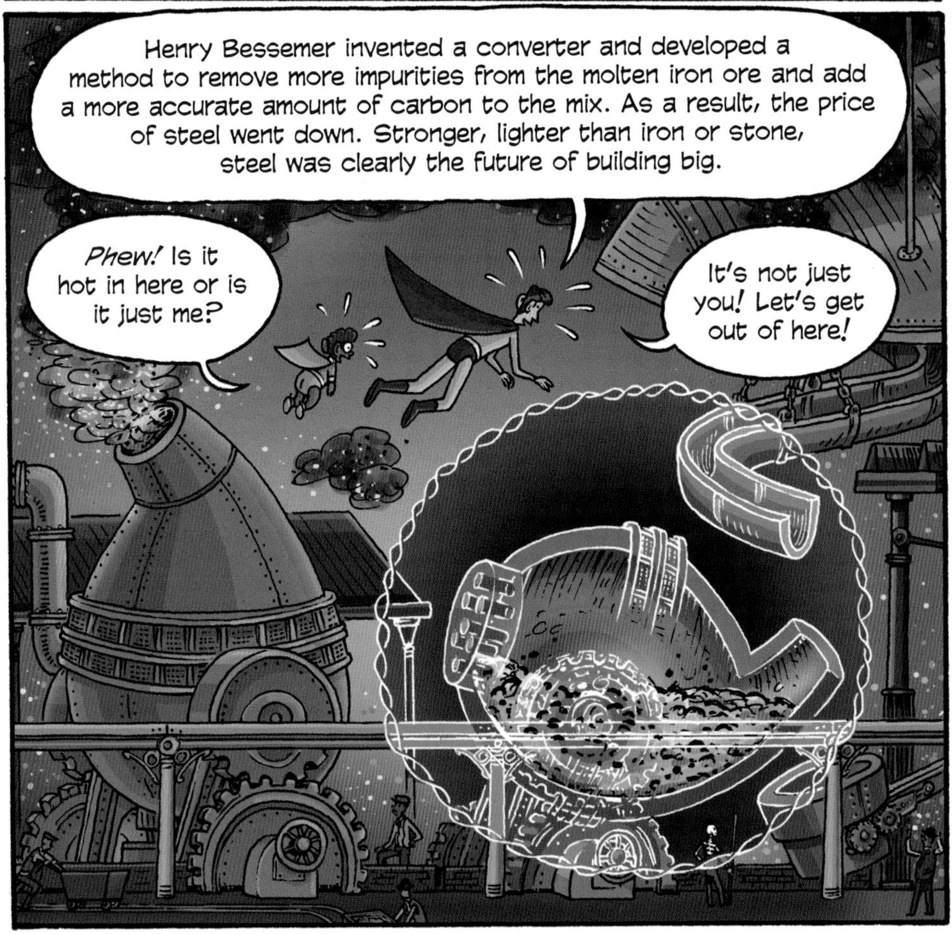
Henry Bessemer invented a converter and developed a method to remove more impurities from the molten iron ore and add a more accurate amount of carbon to the mix. As a result, the price of steel went down. Stronger, lighter than iron or stone, steel was clearly the future of building big.
Phew! Is it hot in here or is it just me?
It's not just you! Let's get out of here!

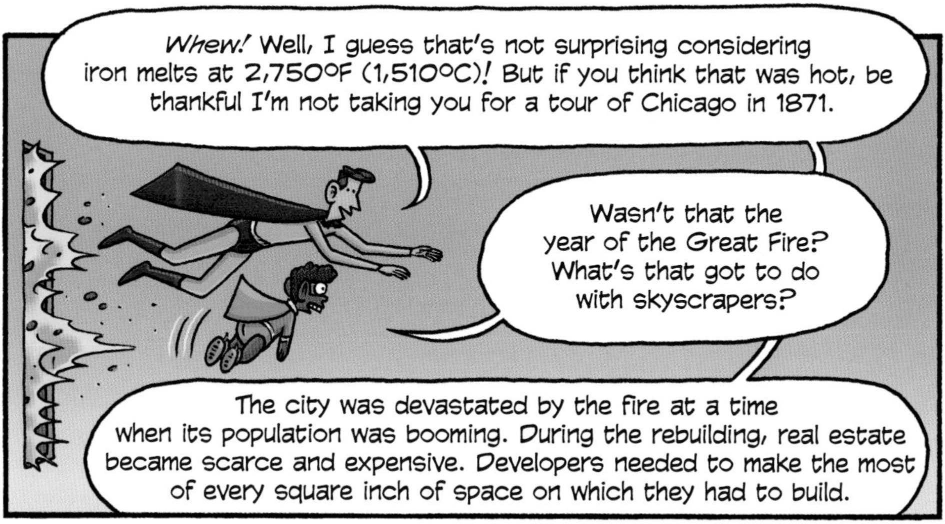
Whew! Well, I guess that's not surprising considering iron melts at 2,750°F (1,510°C)! But if you think that was hot, be thankful I'm not taking you for a tour of Chicago in 1871.
Wasn't that the year of the Great Fire? What's that got to do with skyscrapers?
The city was devastated by the fire at a time when its population was booming. During the rebuilding, real estate became scarce and expensive. Developers needed to make the most of every square inch of space on which they had to build.

There was only one way to go and that was ***up!*** So in 1884, armed with ample knowledge, sturdy materials, and the proper motivation, designer ***William Le Baron Jenney*** took a newly developing approach to building and pushed it to the forefront of construction, the Home Insurance Building.

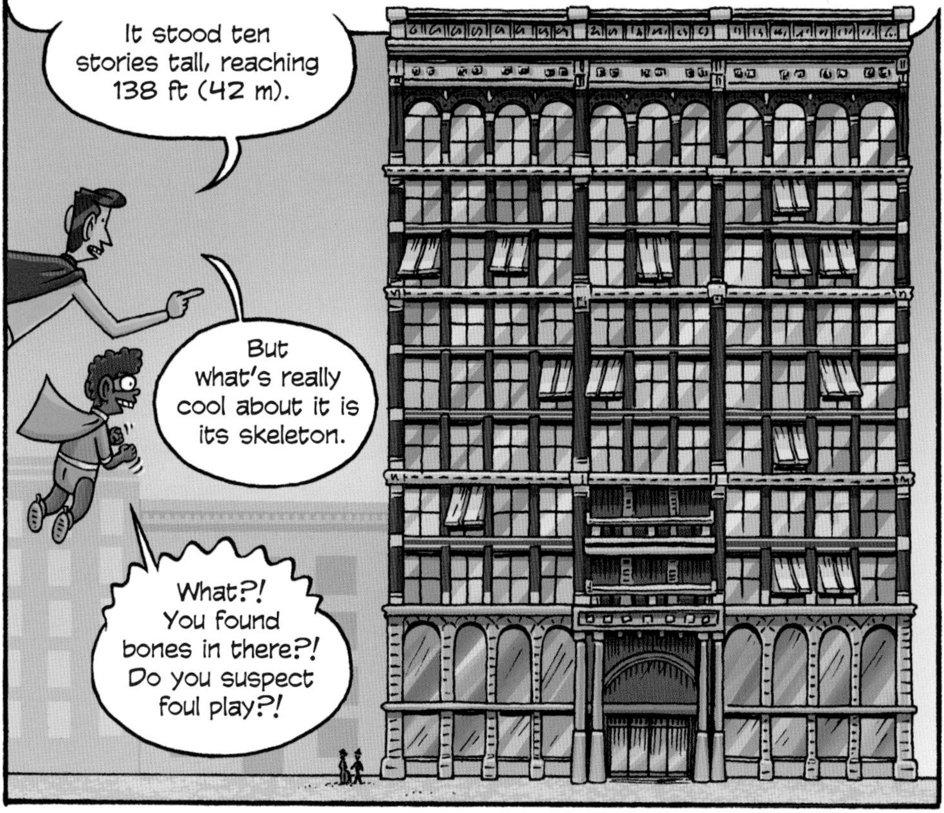
It stood ten stories tall, reaching 138 ft (42 m).
But what's really cool about it is its skeleton.
What?! You found bones in there?! Do you suspect foul play?!

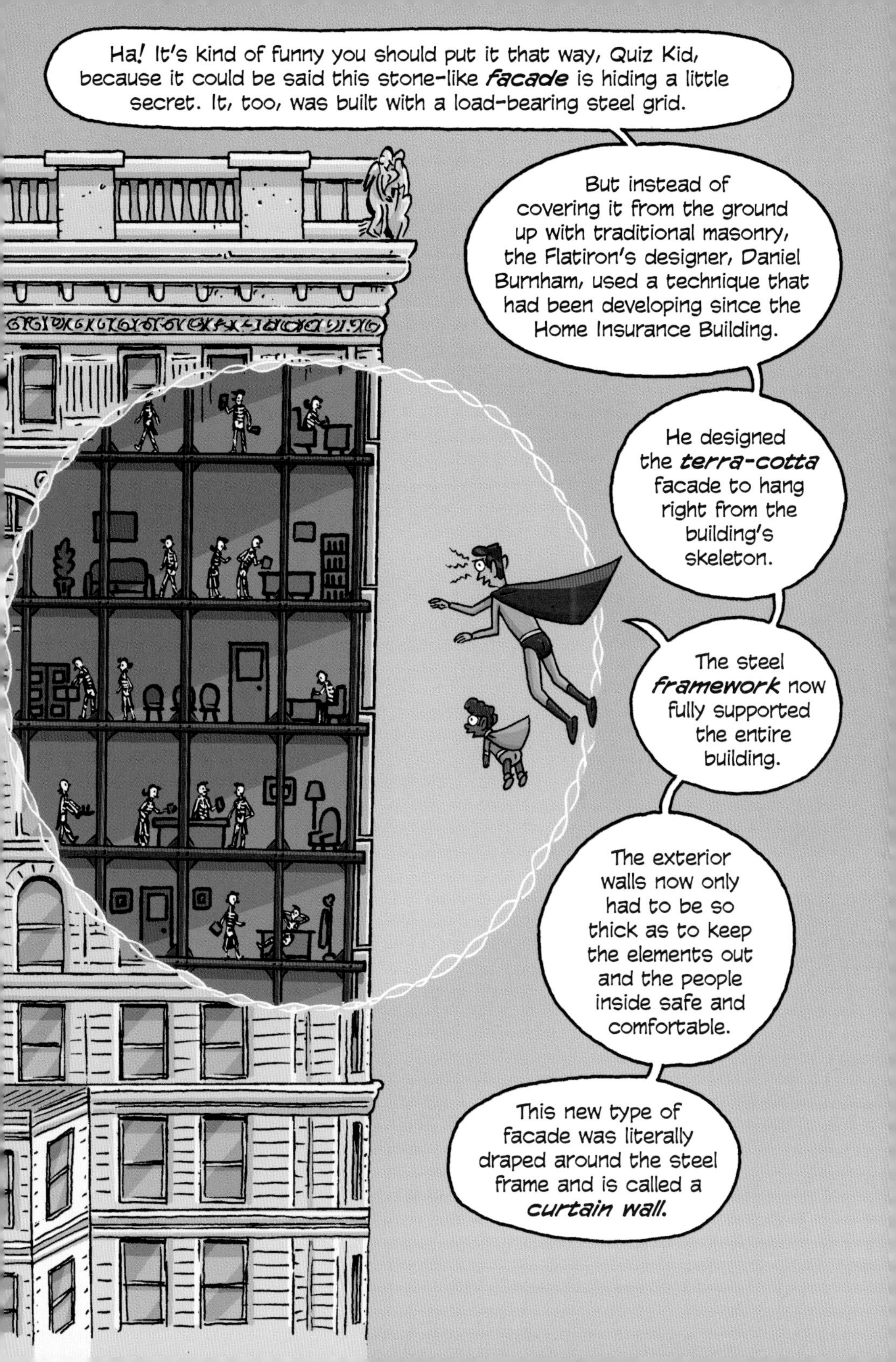
Ha! It's kind of funny you should put it that way, Quiz Kid, because it could be said this stone-like *facade* is hiding a little secret. It, too, was built with a load-bearing steel grid.
But instead of covering it from the ground up with traditional masonry, the Flatiron's designer, Daniel Burnham, used a technique that had been developing since the Home Insurance Building.
He designed the *terra-cotta* facade to hang right from the building's skeleton.
The steel *framework* now fully supported the entire building.
The exterior walls now only had to be so thick as to keep the elements out and the people inside safe and comfortable.
This new type of facade was literally draped around the steel frame and is called a *curtain wall.*

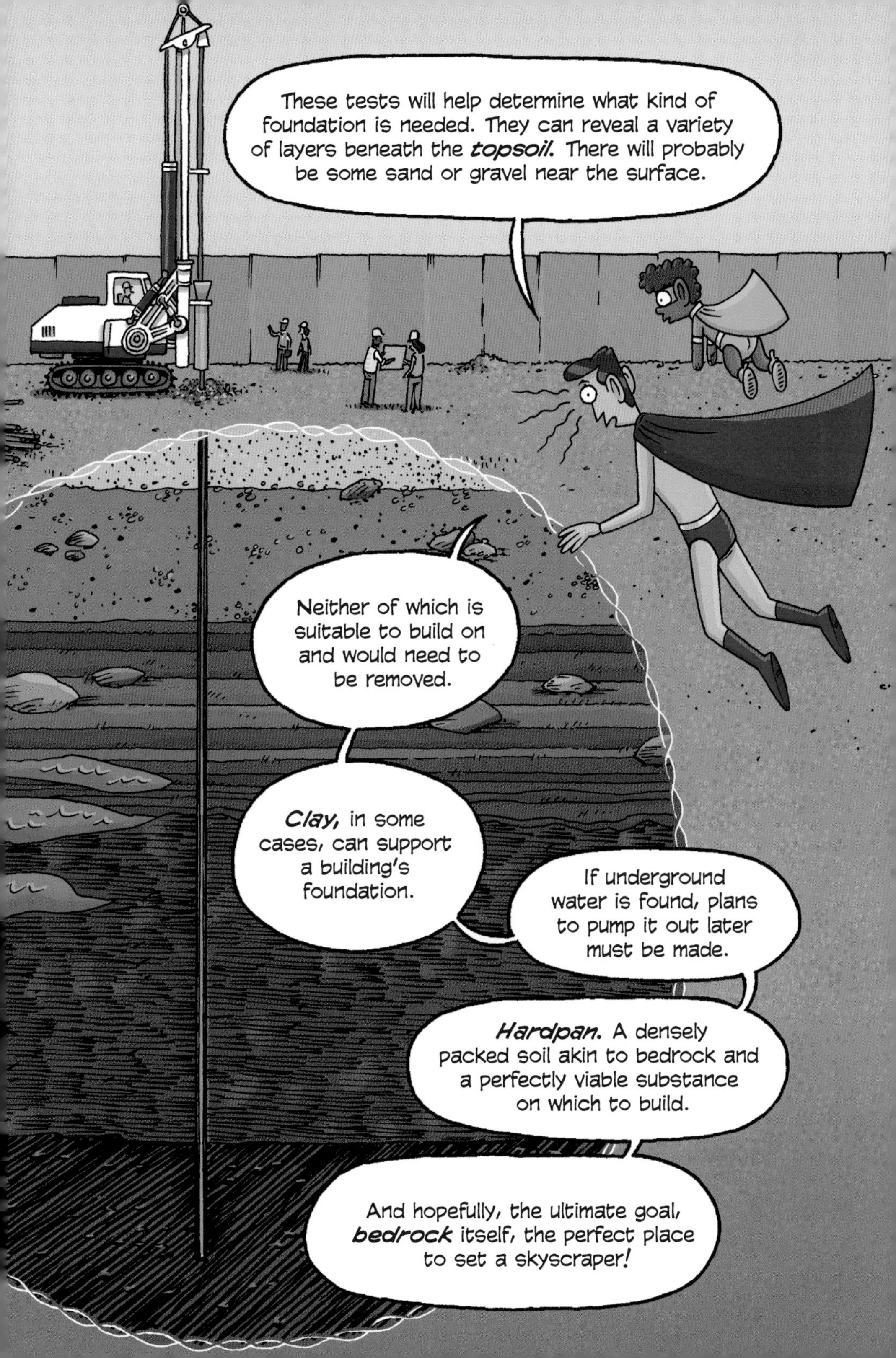
These tests will help determine what kind of foundation is needed. They can reveal a variety of layers beneath the *topsoil.* There will probably be some sand or gravel near the surface.
Neither of which is suitable to build on and would need to be removed.
Clay, in some cases, can support a building's foundation.
If underground water is found, plans to pump it out later must be made.
Hardpan. A densely packed soil akin to bedrock and a perfectly viable substance on which to build.
And hopefully, the ultimate goal, *bedrock* itself, the perfect place to set a skyscraper!

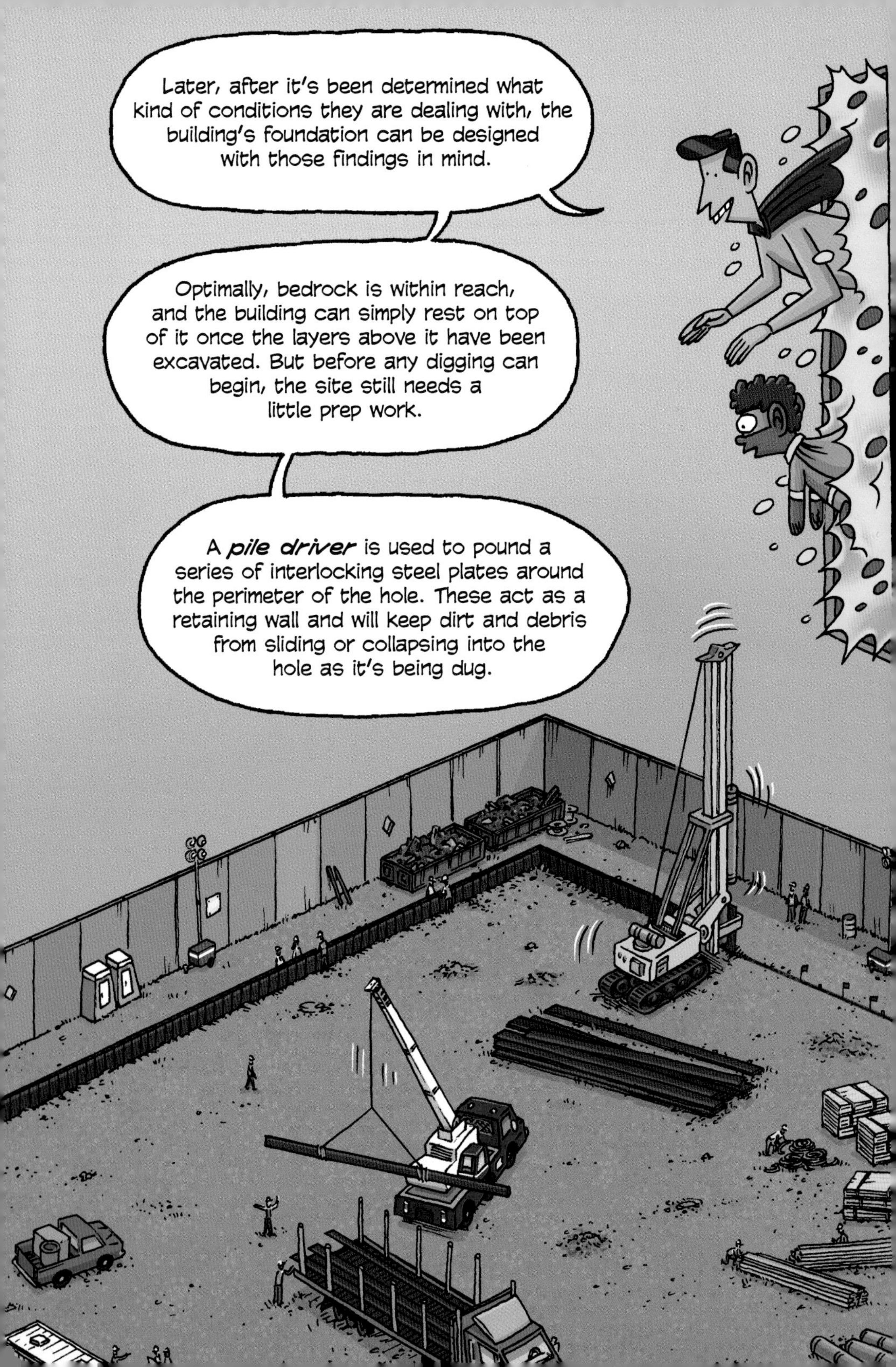
Later, after it's been determined what kind of conditions they are dealing with, the building's foundation can be designed with those findings in mind.
Optimally, bedrock is within reach, and the building can simply rest on top of it once the layers above it have been excavated. But before any digging can begin, the site still needs a little prep work.
A *pile driver* is used to pound a series of interlocking steel plates around the perimeter of the hole. These act as a retaining wall and will keep dirt and debris from sliding or collapsing into the hole as it's being dug.

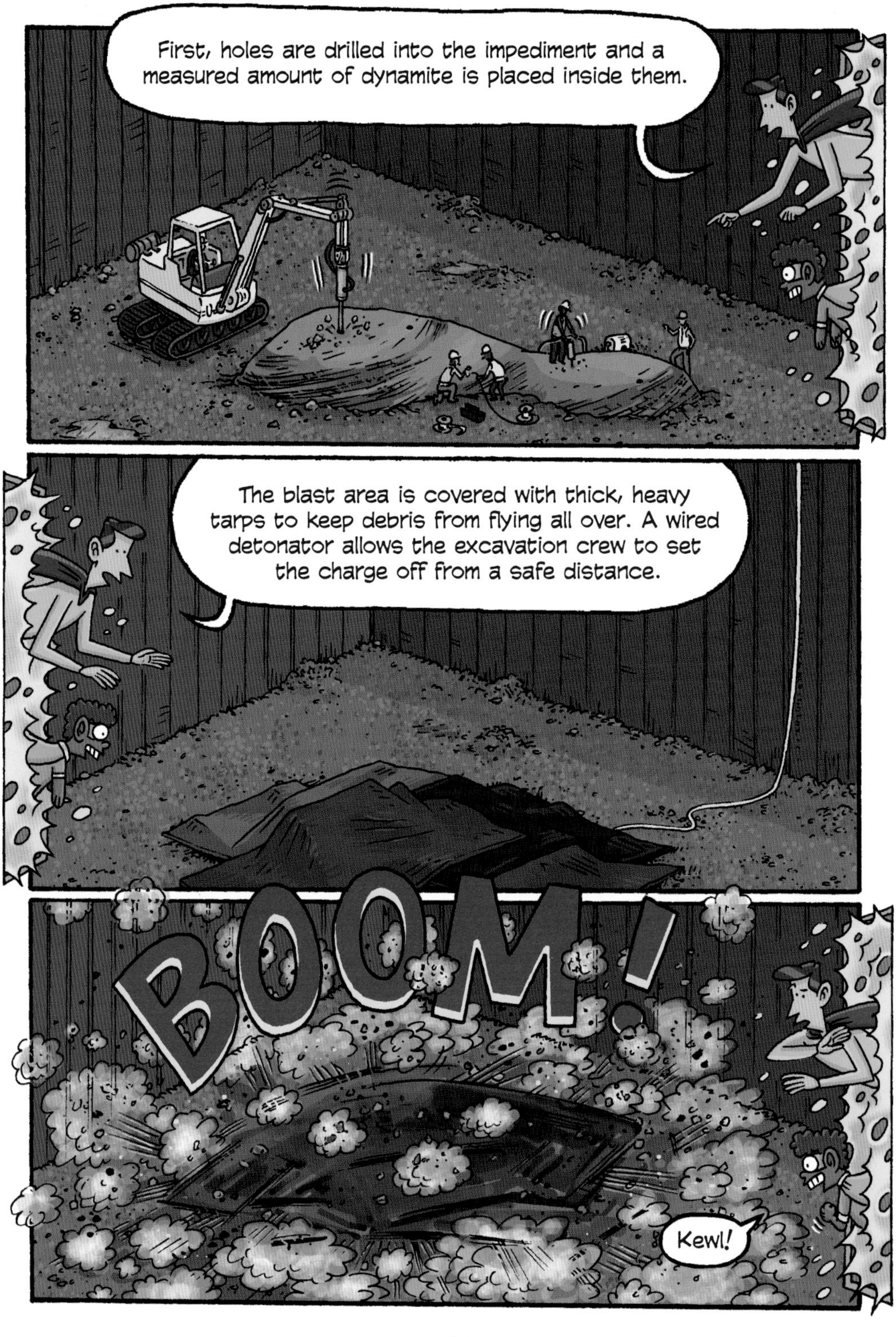
First, holes are drilled into the impediment and a measured amount of dynamite is placed inside them.
The blast area is covered with thick, heavy tarps to keep debris from flying all over. A wired detonator allows the excavation crew to set the charge off from a safe distance.
BOOM!
Kewl!

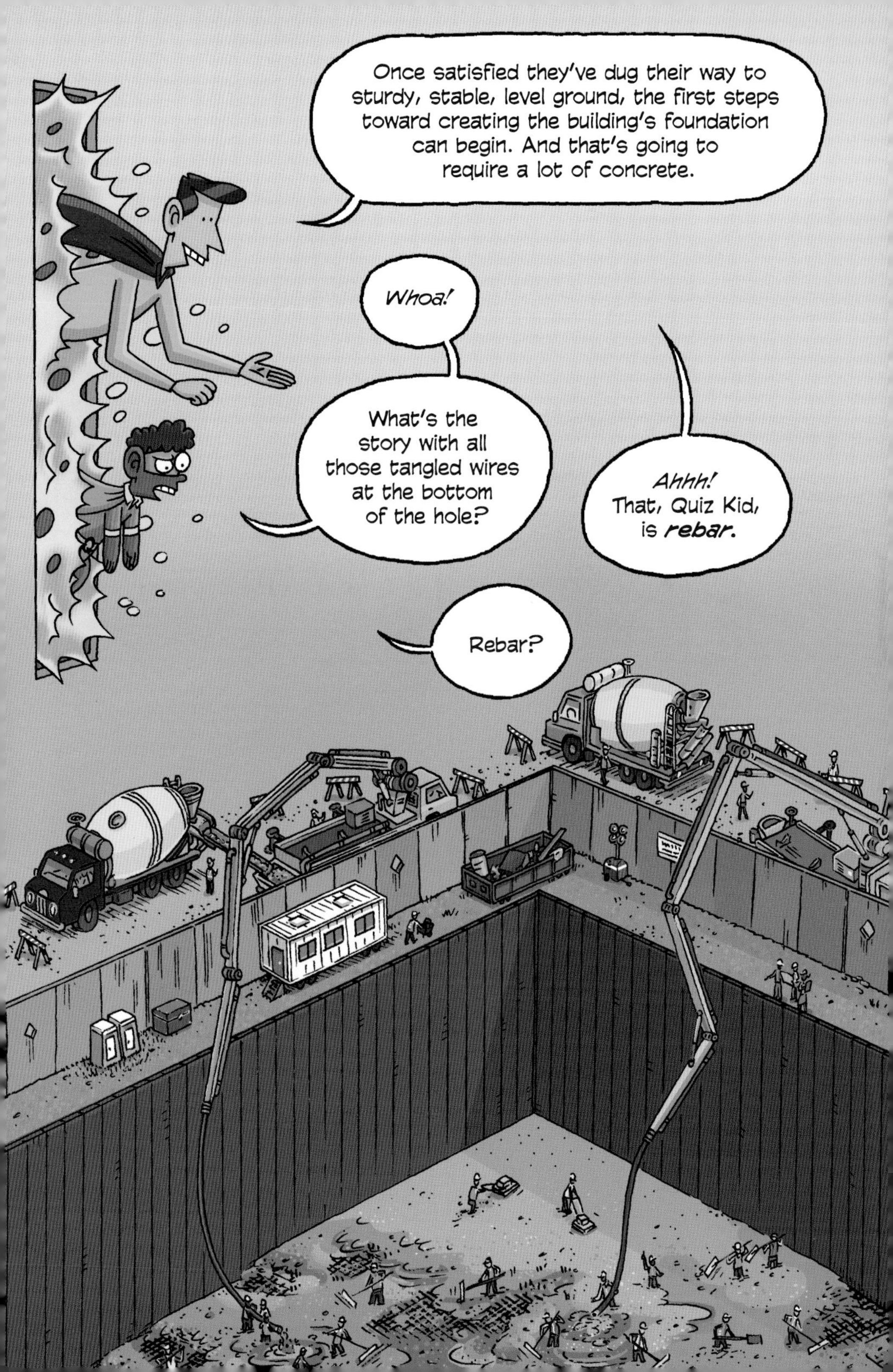
Once satisfied they've dug their way to sturdy, stable, level ground, the first steps toward creating the building's foundation can begin. And that's going to require a lot of concrete.
Whoa!
What's the story with all those tangled wires at the bottom of the hole?
Ahhh! That, Quiz Kid, is ***rebar***.
Rebar?

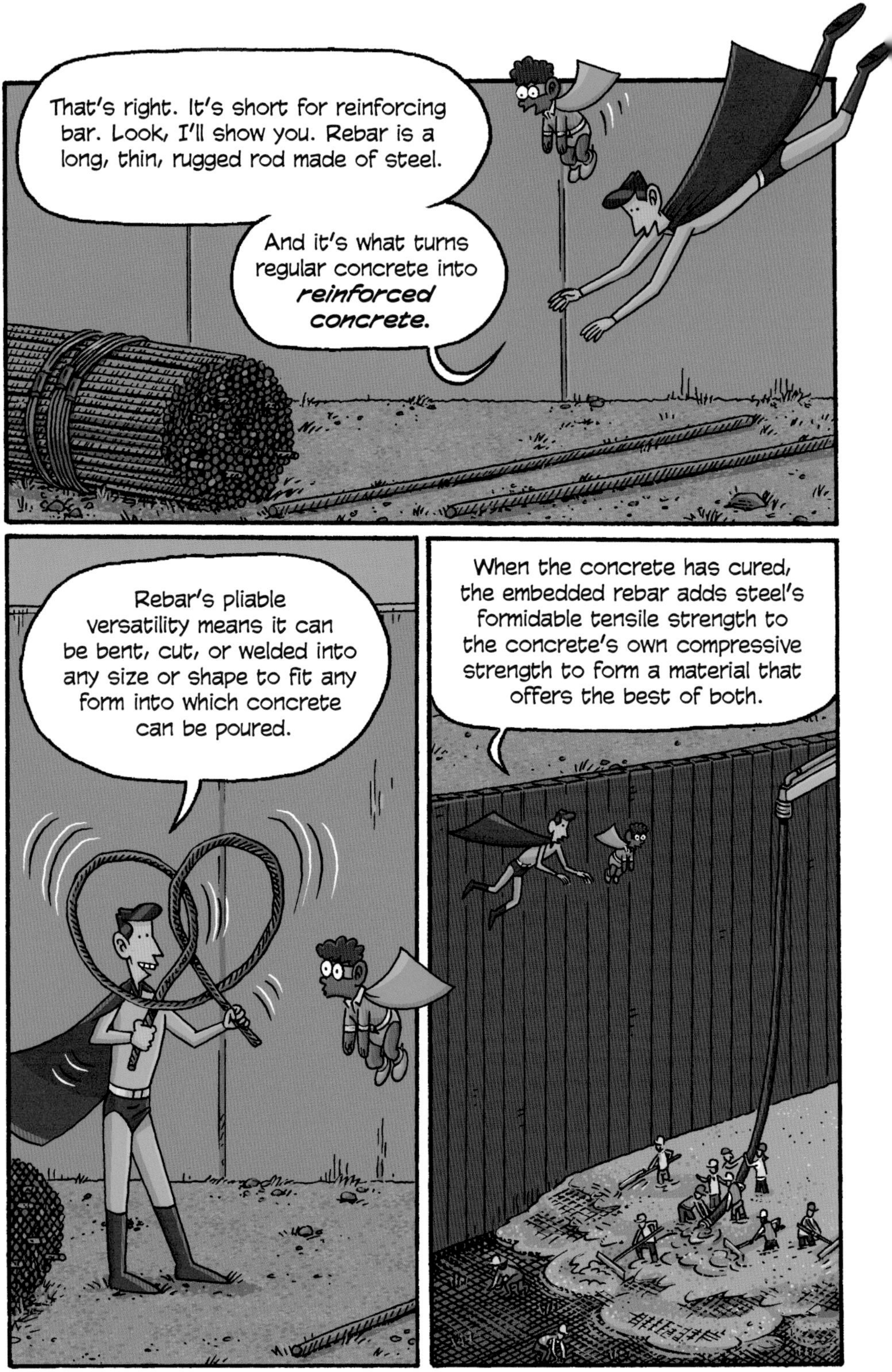
That's right. It's short for reinforcing bar. Look, I'll show you. Rebar is a long, thin, rugged rod made of steel.
And it's what turns regular concrete into *reinforced concrete.*
Rebar's pliable versatility means it can be bent, cut, or welded into any size or shape to fit any form into which concrete can be poured.
When the concrete has cured, the embedded rebar adds steel's formidable tensile strength to the concrete's own compressive strength to form a material that offers the best of both.

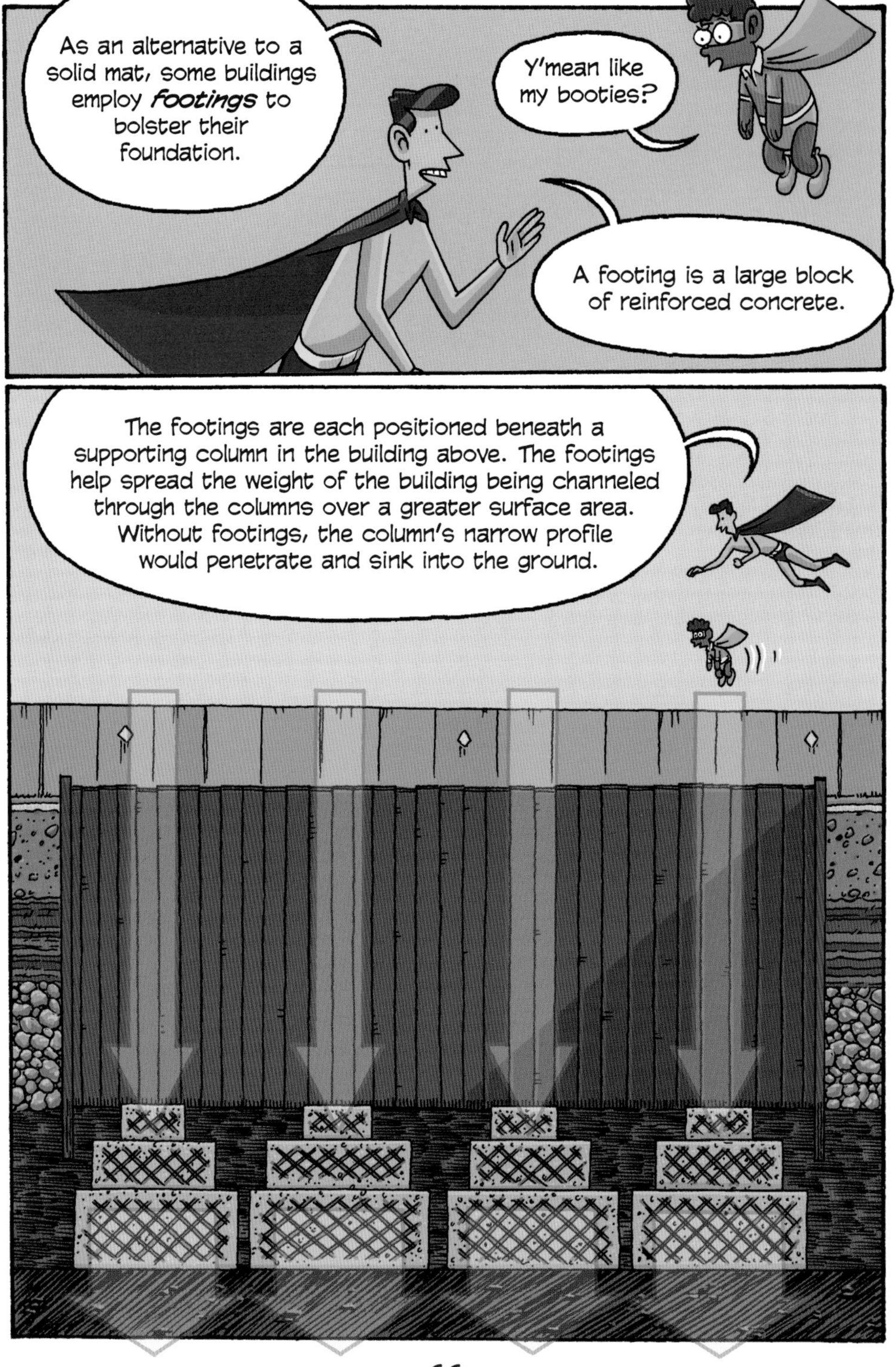
As an alternative to a solid mat, some buildings employ ***footings*** to bolster their foundation.
Y'mean like my booties?
A footing is a large block of reinforced concrete.
The footings are each positioned beneath a supporting column in the building above. The footings help spread the weight of the building being channeled through the columns over a greater surface area. Without footings, the column's narrow profile would penetrate and sink into the ground.

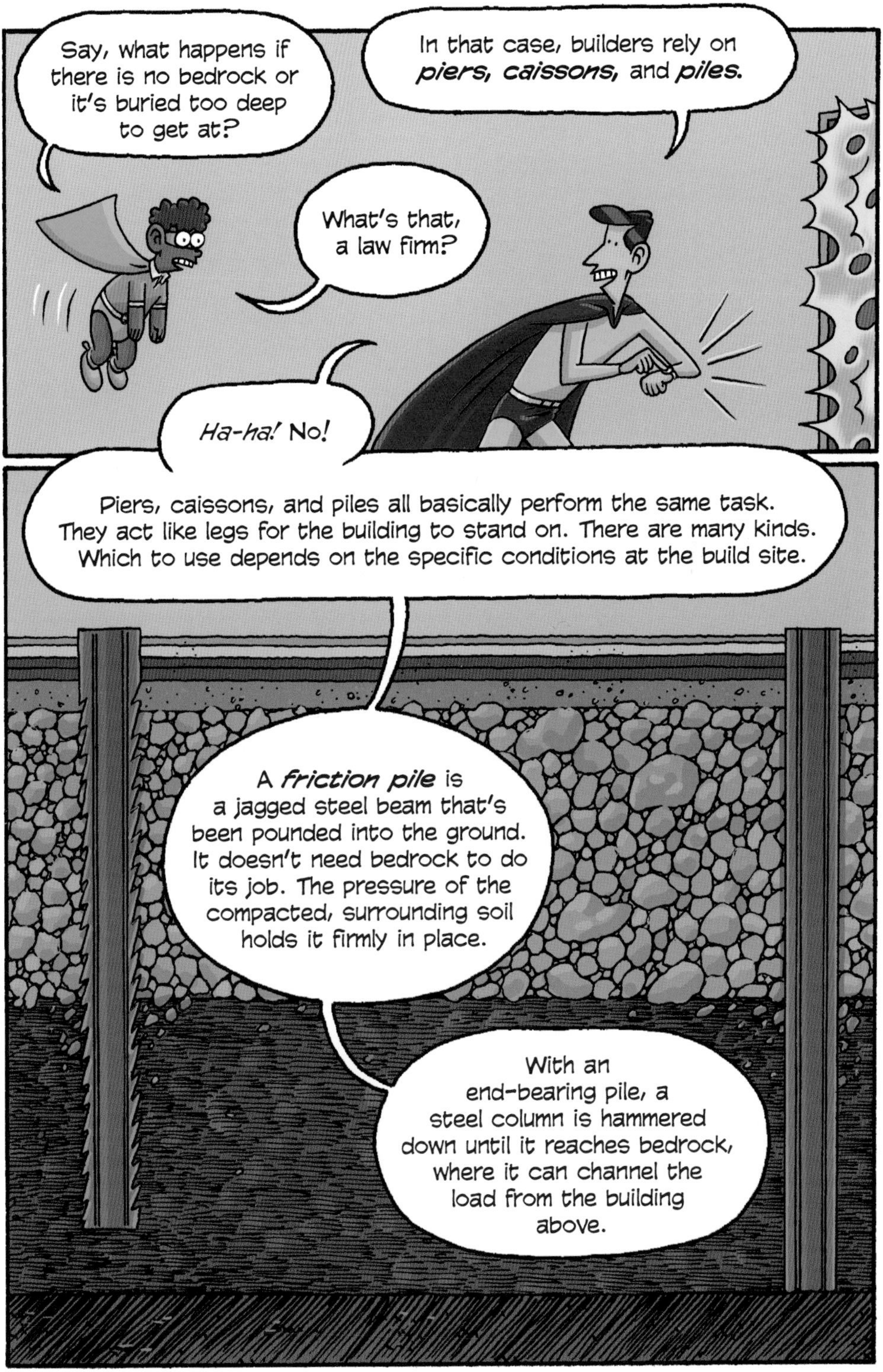

Say, what happens if there is no bedrock or it's buried too deep to get at?
In that case, builders rely on ***piers, caissons,*** and ***piles.***
What's that, a law firm?
Ha-ha! No!
Piers, caissons, and piles all basically perform the same task. They act like legs for the building to stand on. There are many kinds. Which to use depends on the specific conditions at the build site.
A ***friction pile*** is a jagged steel beam that's been pounded into the ground. It doesn't need bedrock to do its job. The pressure of the compacted, surrounding soil holds it firmly in place.
With an end-bearing pile, a steel column is hammered down until it reaches bedrock, where it can channel the load from the building above.

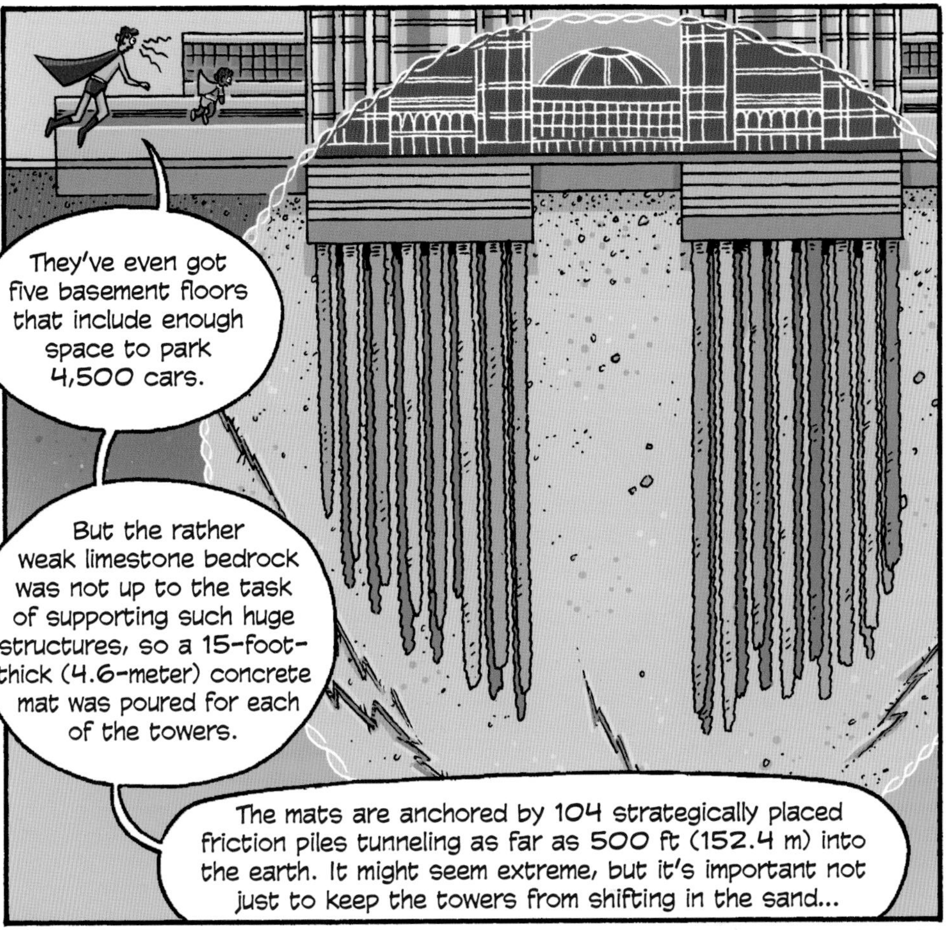
They've even got five basement floors that include enough space to park 4,500 cars.
But the rather weak limestone bedrock was not up to the task of supporting such huge structures, so a 15-foot-thick (4.6-meter) concrete mat was poured for each of the towers.
The mats are anchored by 104 strategically placed friction piles tunneling as far as 500 ft (152.4 m) into the earth. It might seem extreme, but it's important not just to keep the towers from shifting in the sand...

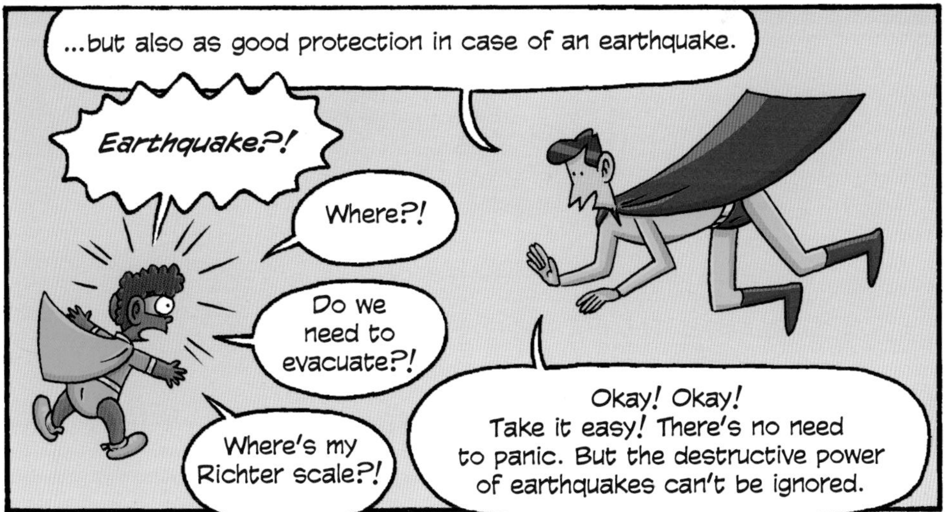
...but also as good protection in case of an earthquake.
Earthquake?!
Where?!
Do we need to evacuate?!
Where's my Richter scale?!
Okay! Okay! Take it easy! There's no need to panic. But the destructive power of earthquakes can't be ignored.

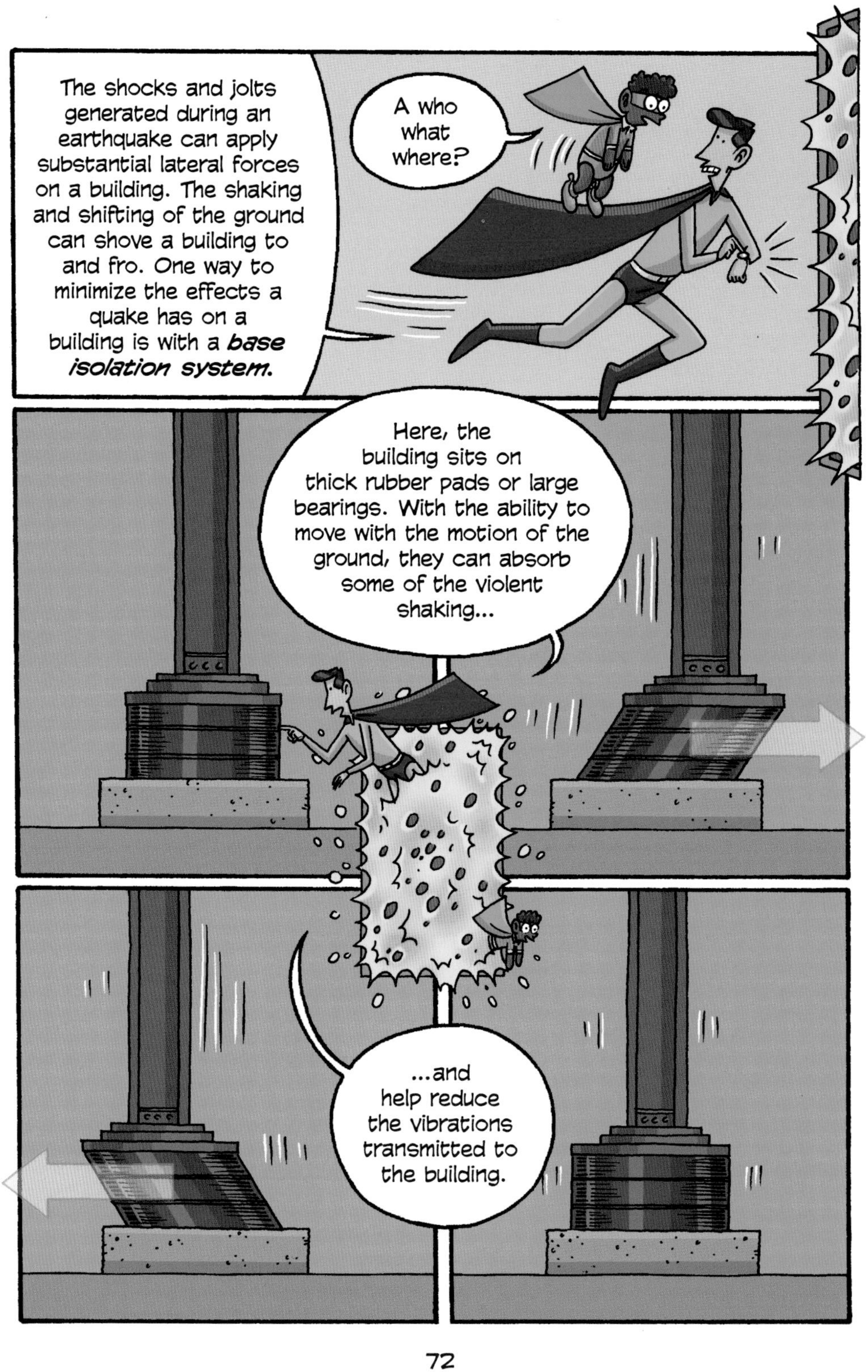
The shocks and jolts generated during an earthquake can apply substantial lateral forces on a building. The shaking and shifting of the ground can shove a building to and fro. One way to minimize the effects a quake has on a building is with a ***base isolation system.***
A who what where?
Here, the building sits on thick rubber pads or large bearings. With the ability to move with the motion of the ground, they can absorb some of the violent shaking...
...and help reduce the vibrations transmitted to the building.

73

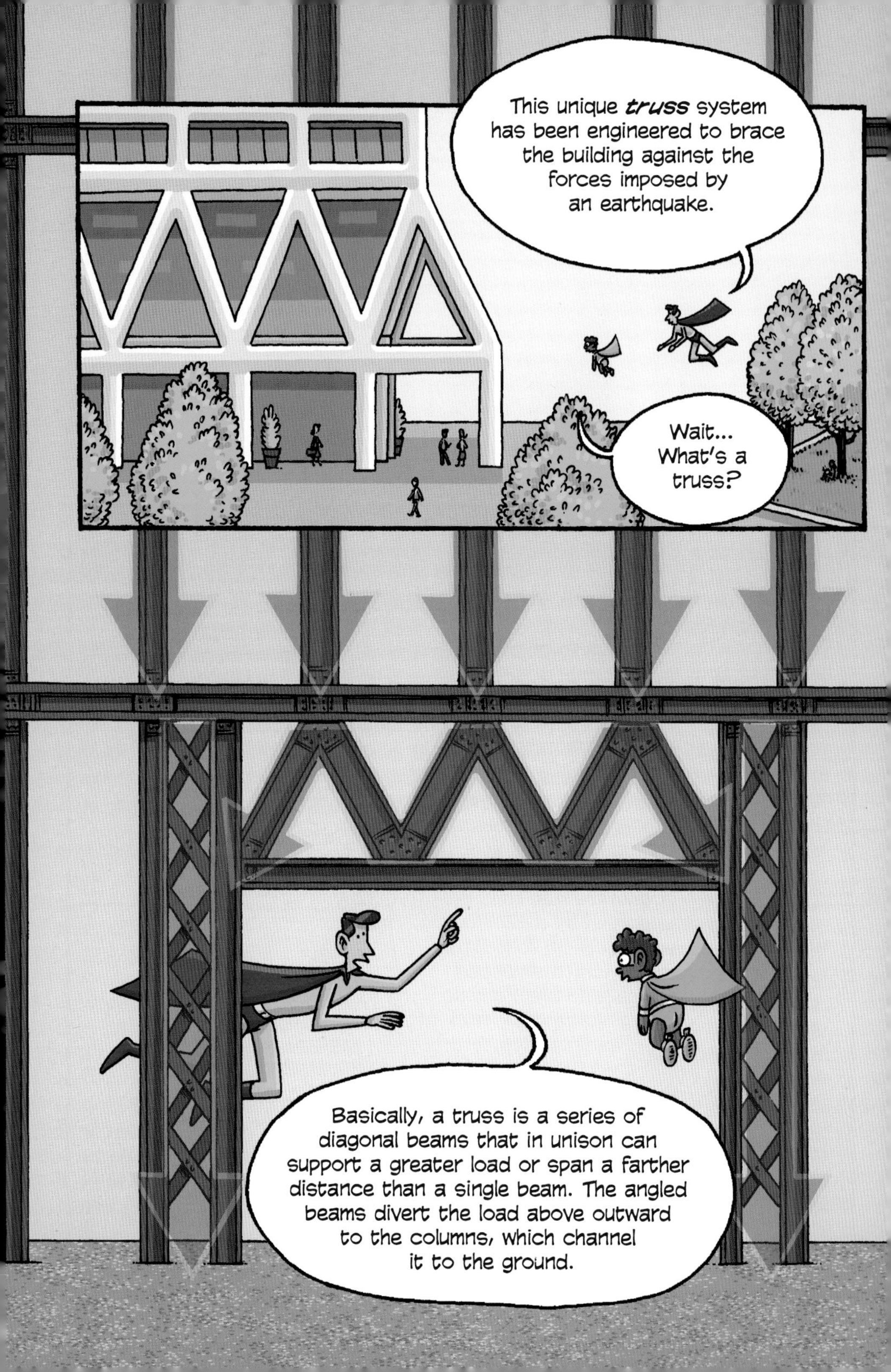
This unique *truss* system has been engineered to brace the building against the forces imposed by an earthquake.
Wait... What's a truss?
Basically, a truss is a series of diagonal beams that in unison can support a greater load or span a farther distance than a single beam. The angled beams divert the load above outward to the columns, which channel it to the ground.

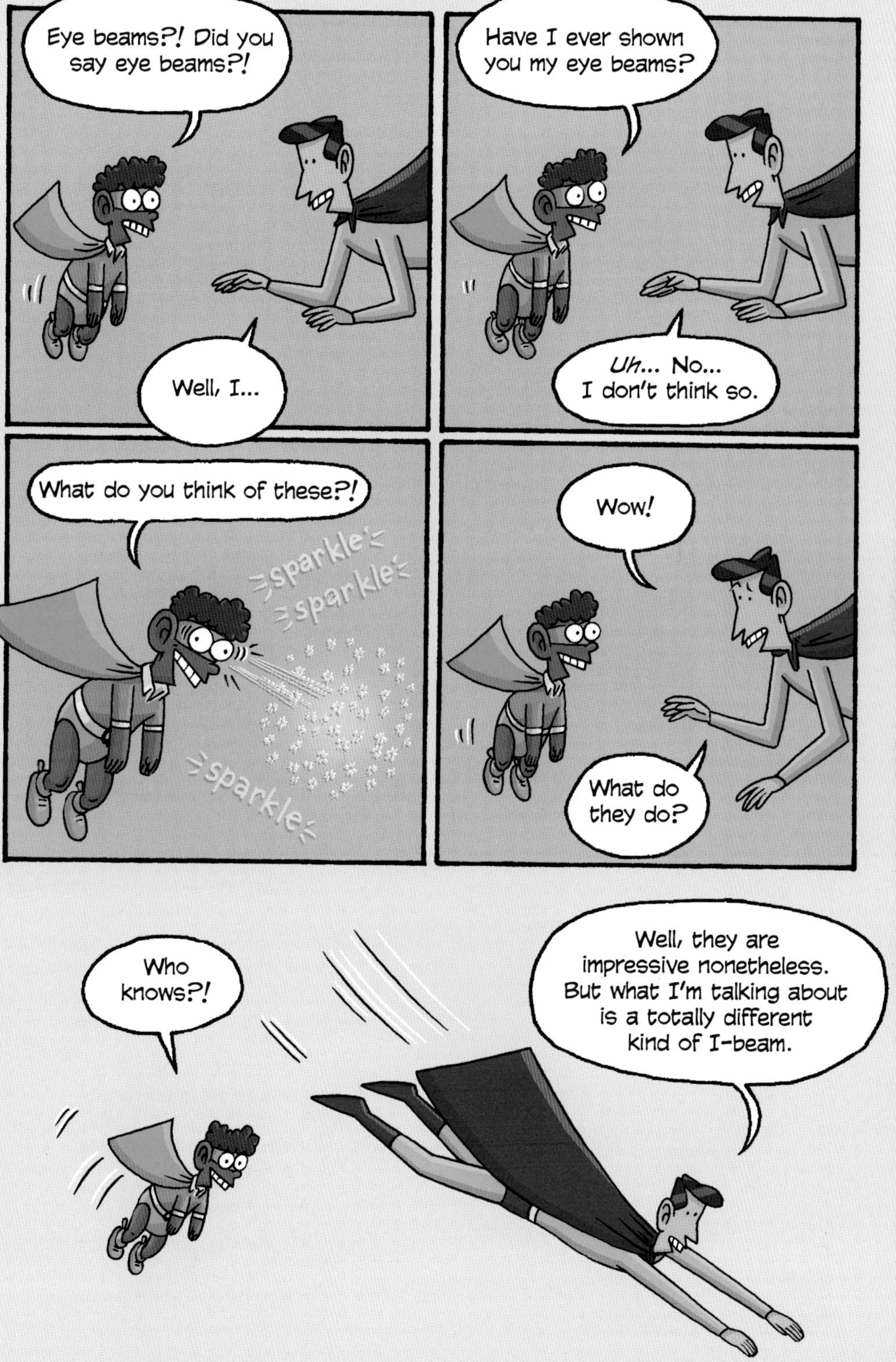

Eye beams?! Did you say eye beams?!
Well, I...
Have I ever shown you my eye beams?
Uh... No... I don't think so.
What do you think of these?!
sparkle
sparkle
sparkle
Wow!
What do they do?
Who knows?!
Well, they are impressive nonetheless. But what I'm talking about is a totally different kind of I-beam.

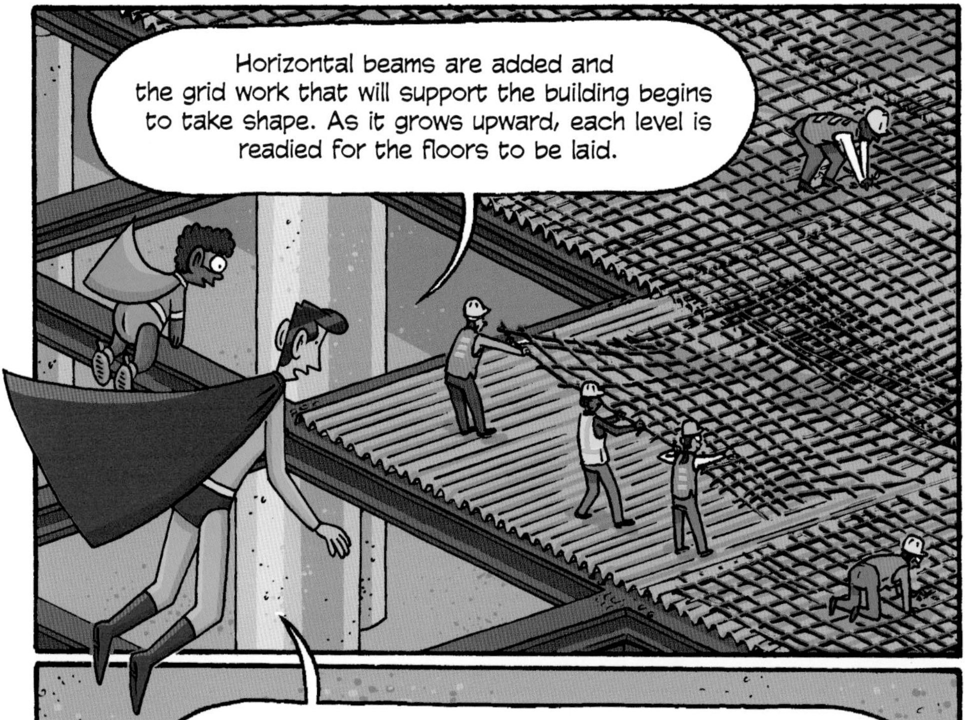
Horizontal beams are added and the grid work that will support the building begins to take shape. As it grows upward, each level is readied for the floors to be laid.

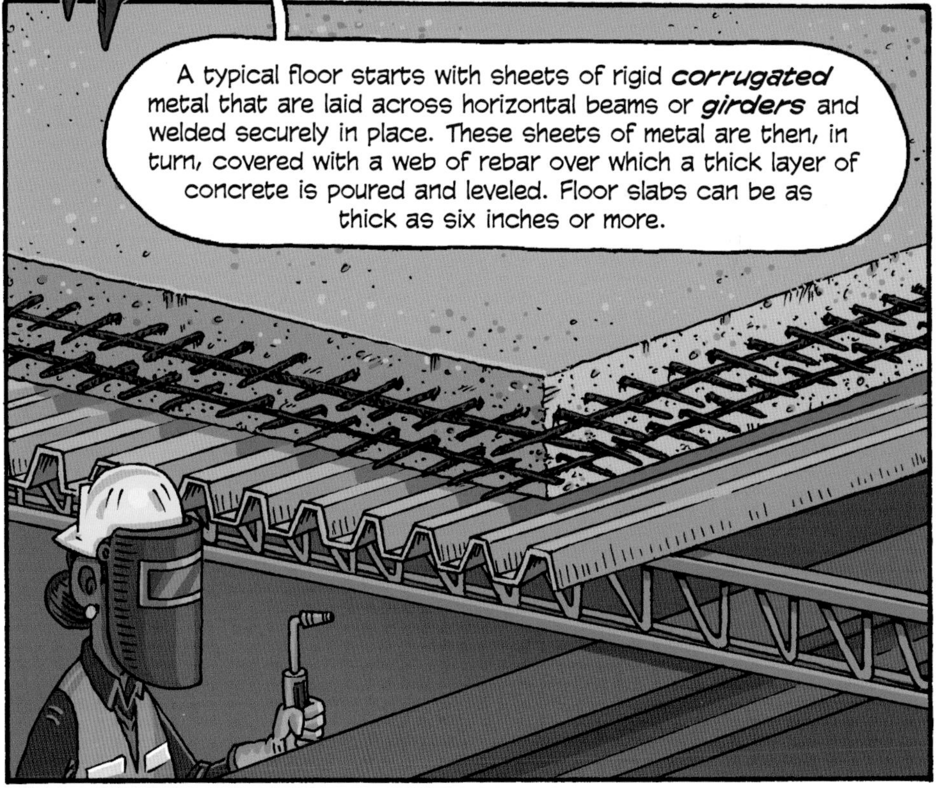
A typical floor starts with sheets of rigid ***corrugated*** metal that are laid across horizontal beams or ***girders*** and welded securely in place. These sheets of metal are then, in turn, covered with a web of rebar over which a thick layer of concrete is poured and leveled. Floor slabs can be as thick as six inches or more.

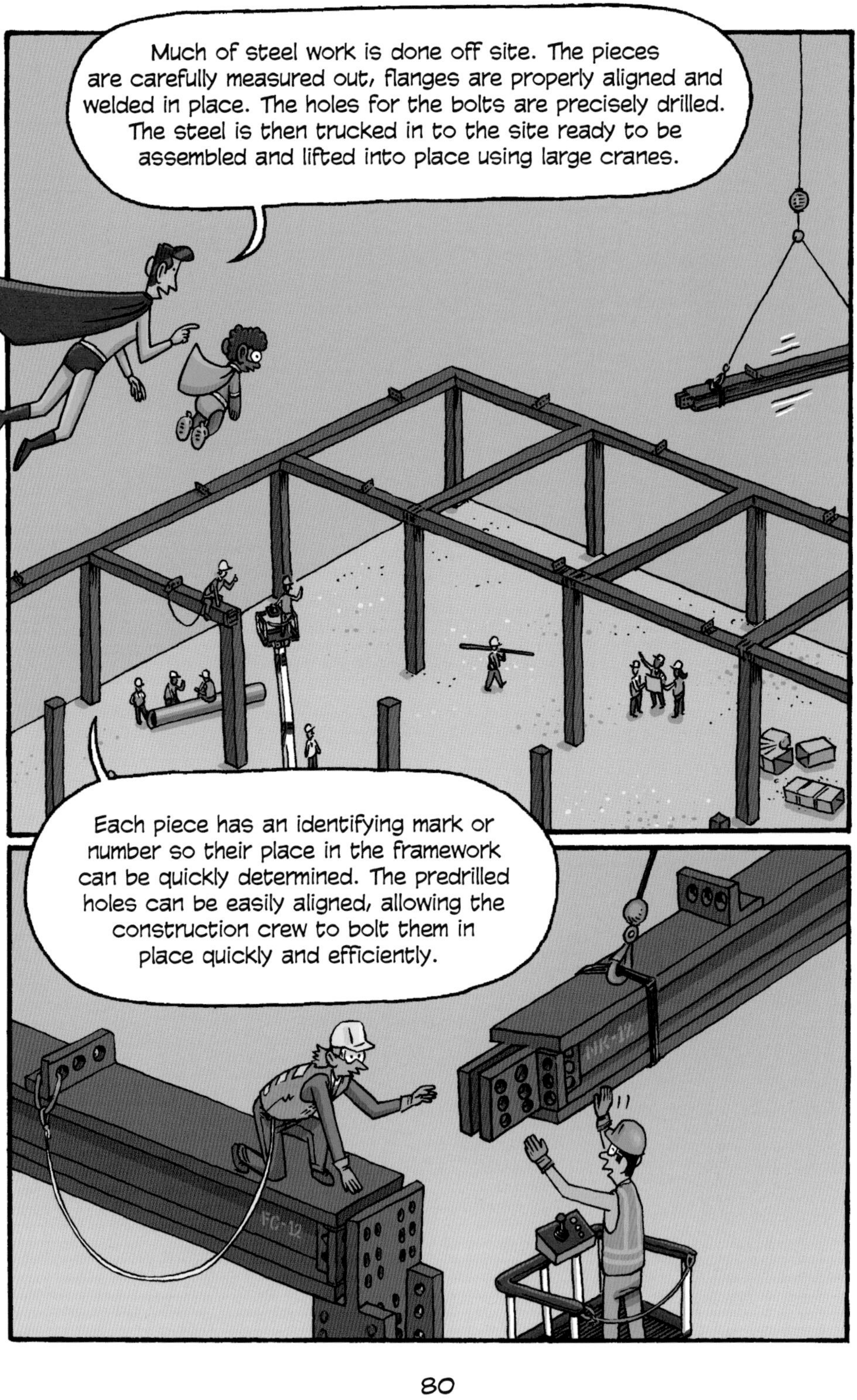
Much of steel work is done off site. The pieces are carefully measured out, flanges are properly aligned and welded in place. The holes for the bolts are precisely drilled. The steel is then trucked in to the site ready to be assembled and lifted into place using large cranes.
Each piece has an identifying mark or number so their place in the framework can be quickly determined. The predrilled holes can be easily aligned, allowing the construction crew to bolt them in place quickly and efficiently.
FC-12

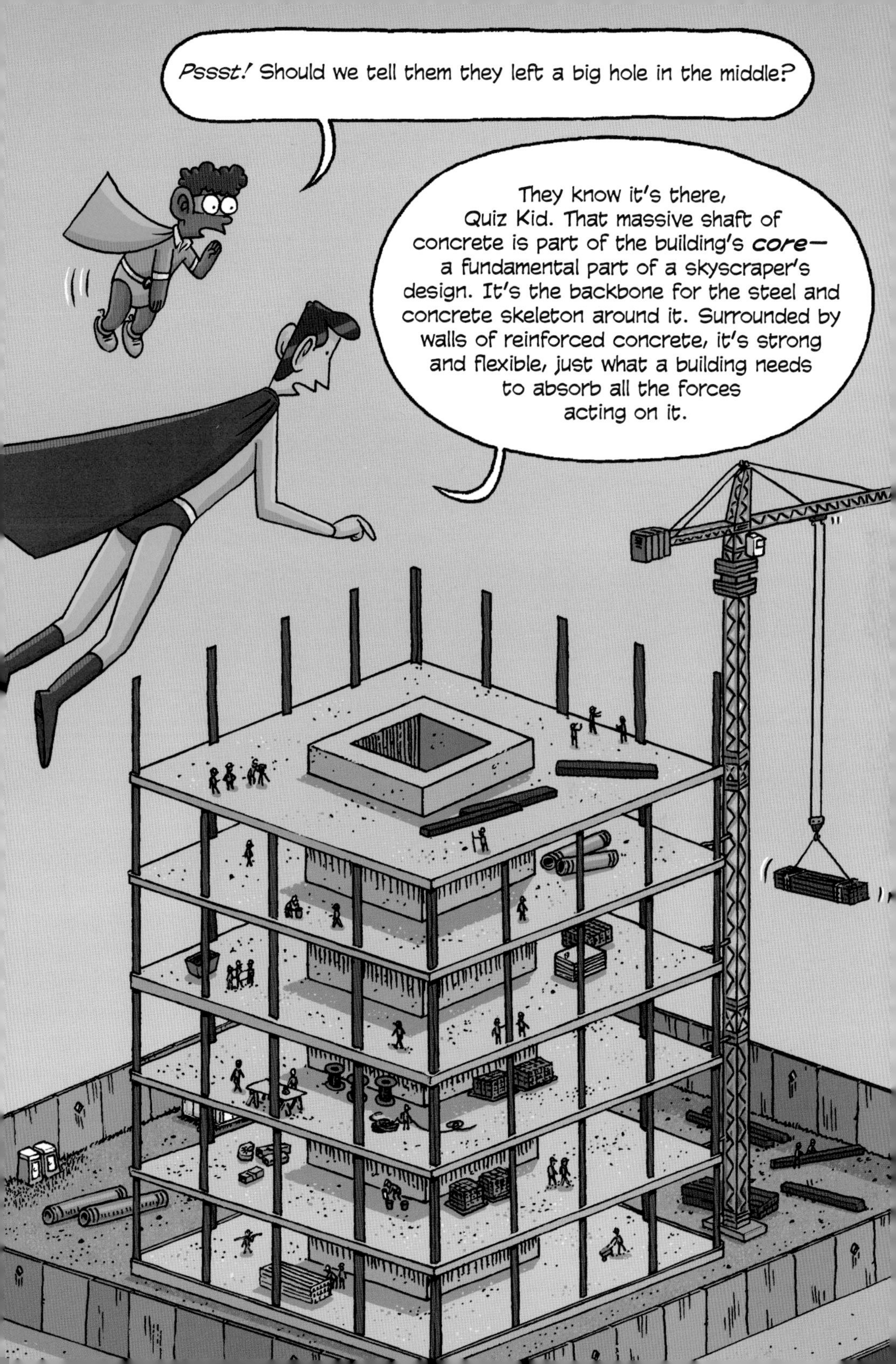

Pssst! Should we tell them they left a big hole in the middle?
They know it's there, Quiz Kid. That massive shaft of concrete is part of the building's ***core***— a fundamental part of a skyscraper's design. It's the backbone for the steel and concrete skeleton around it. Surrounded by walls of reinforced concrete, it's strong and flexible, just what a building needs to absorb all the forces acting on it.

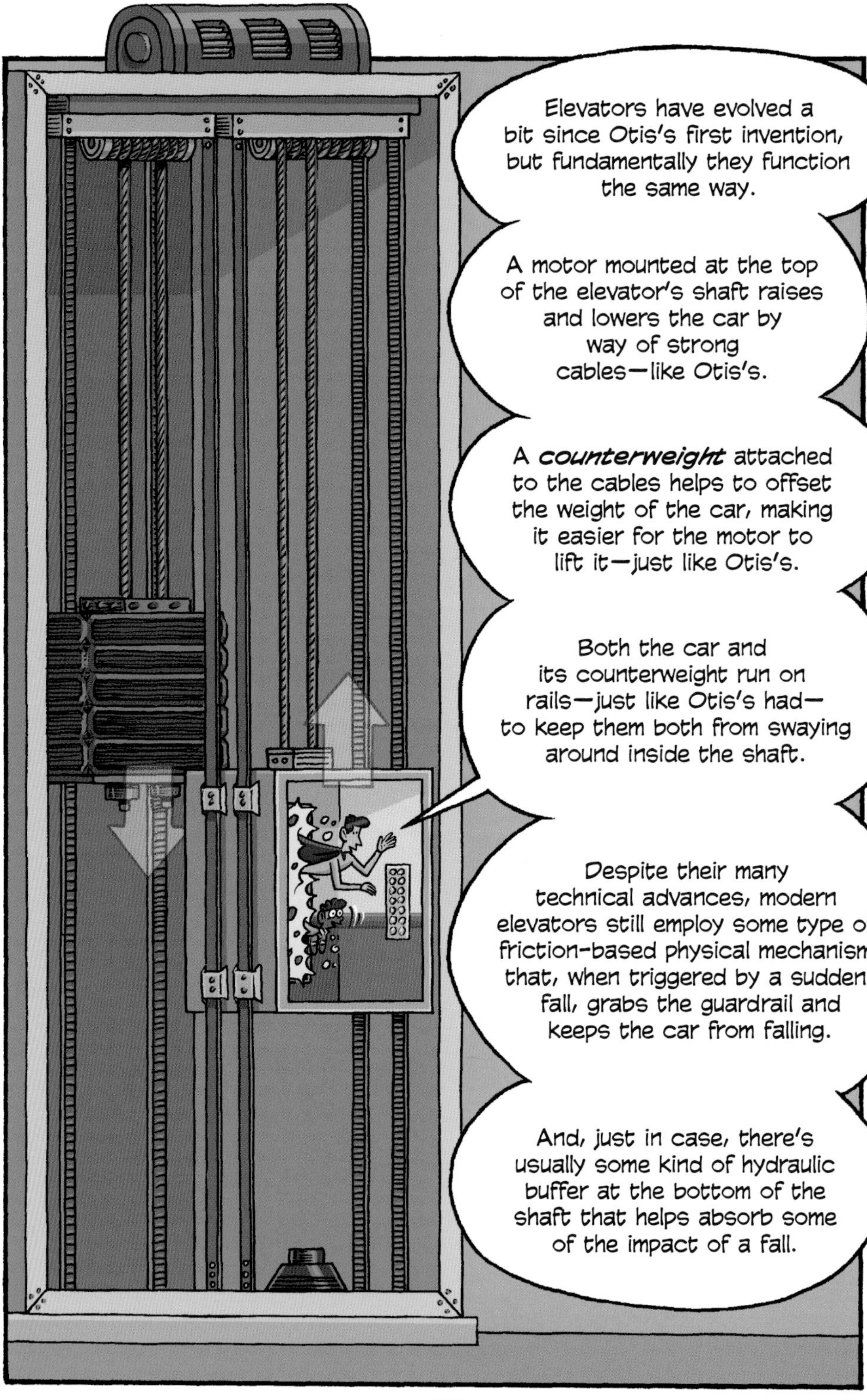
Elevators have evolved a bit since Otis's first invention, but fundamentally they function the same way.
A motor mounted at the top of the elevator's shaft raises and lowers the car by way of strong cables—like Otis's.
A ***counterweight*** attached to the cables helps to offset the weight of the car, making it easier for the motor to lift it—just like Otis's.
Both the car and its counterweight run on rails—just like Otis's had—to keep them both from swaying around inside the shaft.
Despite their many technical advances, modern elevators still employ some type of friction-based physical mechanism that, when triggered by a sudden fall, grabs the guardrail and keeps the car from falling.
And, just in case, there's usually some kind of hydraulic buffer at the bottom of the shaft that helps absorb some of the impact of a fall.

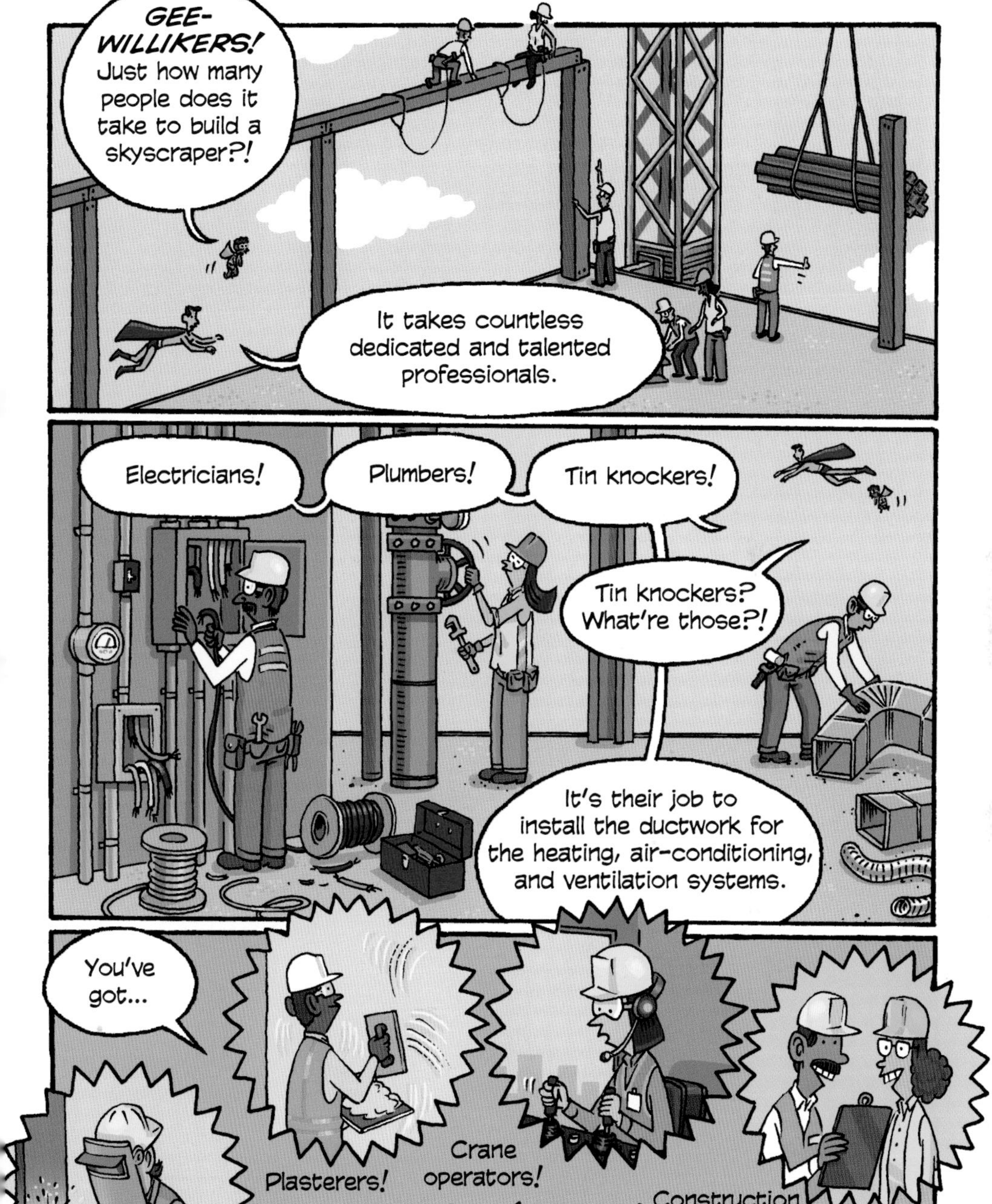
GEE-WILLIKERS! Just how many people does it take to build a skyscraper?!
It takes countless dedicated and talented professionals.
Electricians!
Plumbers!
Tin knockers!
Tin knockers? What're those?!
It's their job to install the ductwork for the heating, air-conditioning, and ventilation systems.
You've got...
Welders!
Inspectors!
Plasterers!
Painters!
Crane operators!
Bolt tighteners!
Masons!
Construction managers!
Am I supposed to say "When"?

89

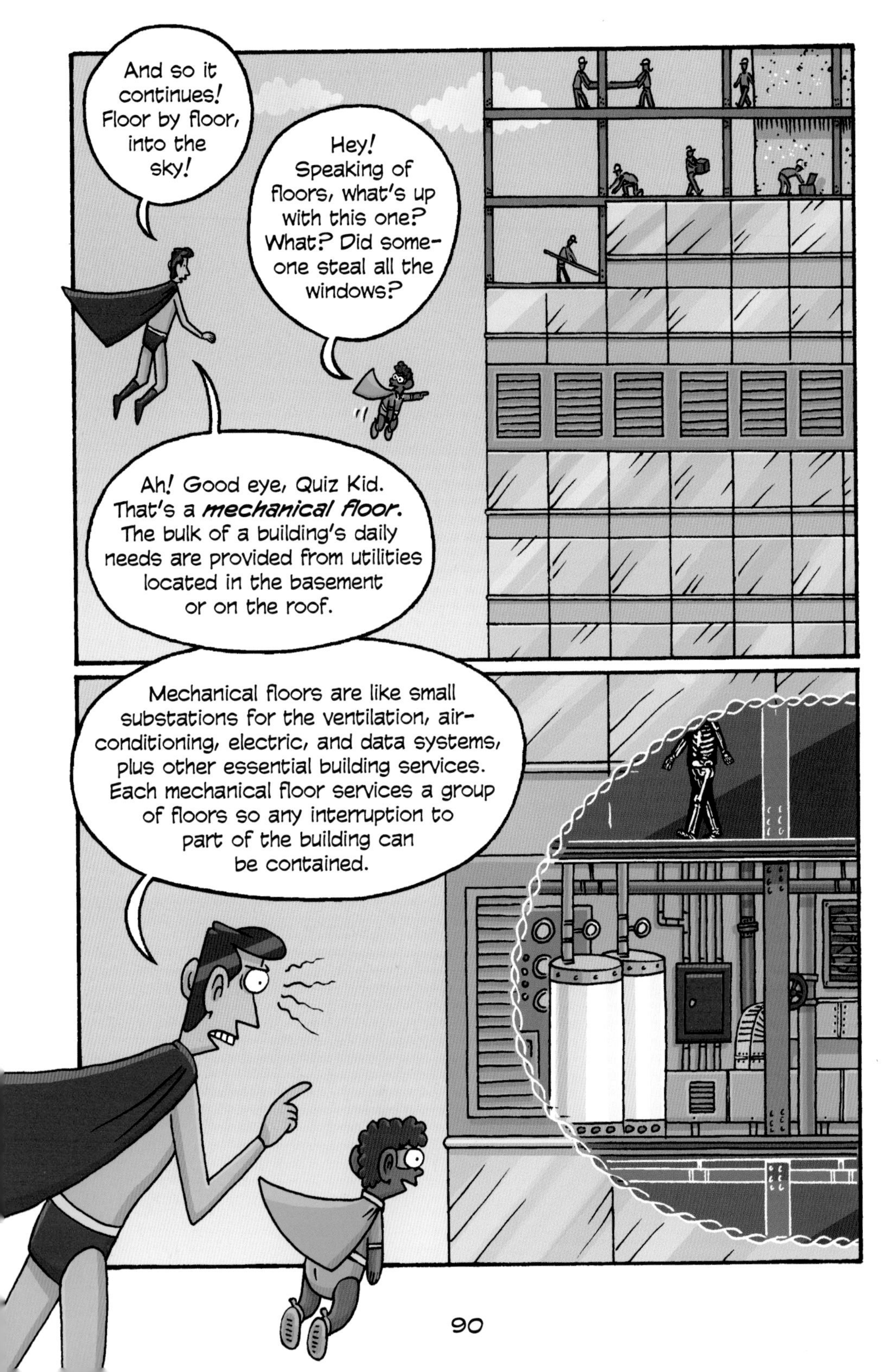

And so it continues! Floor by floor, into the sky!
Hey! Speaking of floors, what's up with this one? What? Did some-one steal all the windows?
Ah! Good eye, Quiz Kid. That's a ***mechanical floor.*** The bulk of a building's daily needs are provided from utilities located in the basement or on the roof.
Mechanical floors are like small substations for the ventilation, air-conditioning, electric, and data systems, plus other essential building services. Each mechanical floor services a group of floors so any interruption to part of the building can be contained.

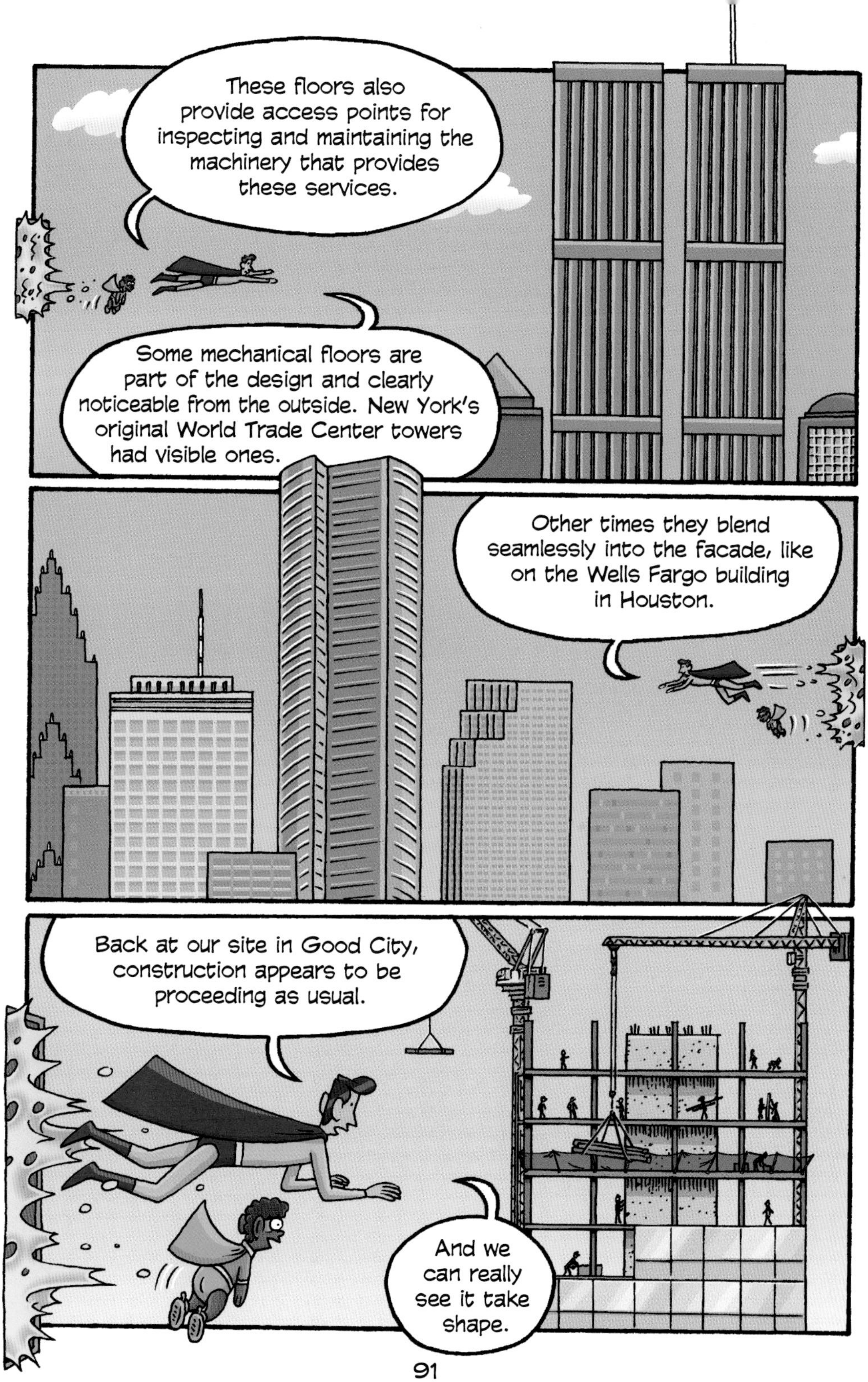
These floors also provide access points for inspecting and maintaining the machinery that provides these services.
Some mechanical floors are part of the design and clearly noticeable from the outside. New York's original World Trade Center towers had visible ones.
Other times they blend seamlessly into the facade, like on the Wells Fargo building in Houston.
Back at our site in Good City, construction appears to be proceeding as usual.
And we can really see it take shape.

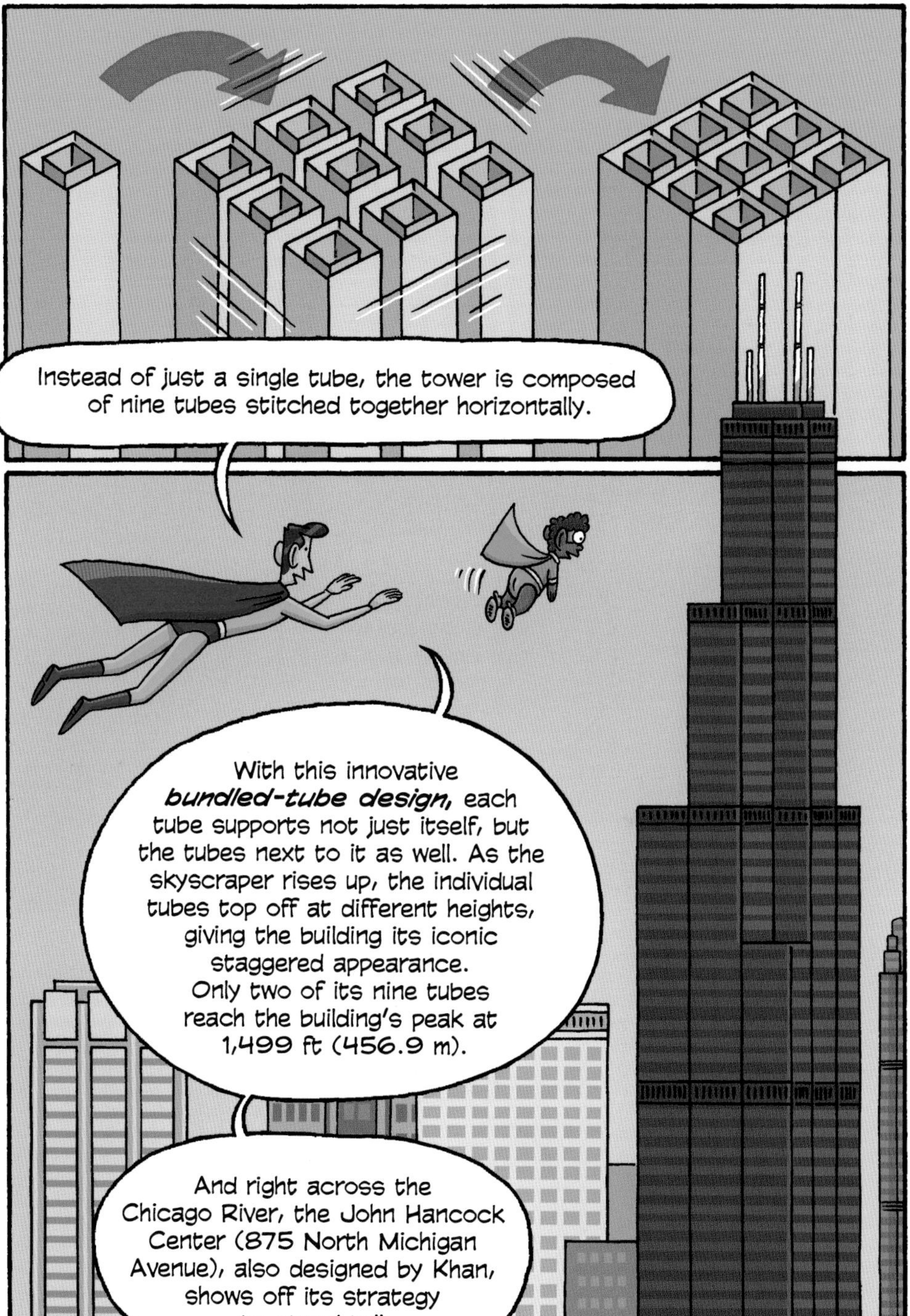
Instead of just a single tube, the tower is composed of nine tubes stitched together horizontally.
With this innovative ***bundled-tube design,*** each tube supports not just itself, but the tubes next to it as well. As the skyscraper rises up, the individual tubes top off at different heights, giving the building its iconic staggered appearance. Only two of its nine tubes reach the building's peak at 1,499 ft (456.9 m).
And right across the Chicago River, the John Hancock Center (875 North Michigan Avenue), also designed by Khan, shows off its strategy to stand tall.

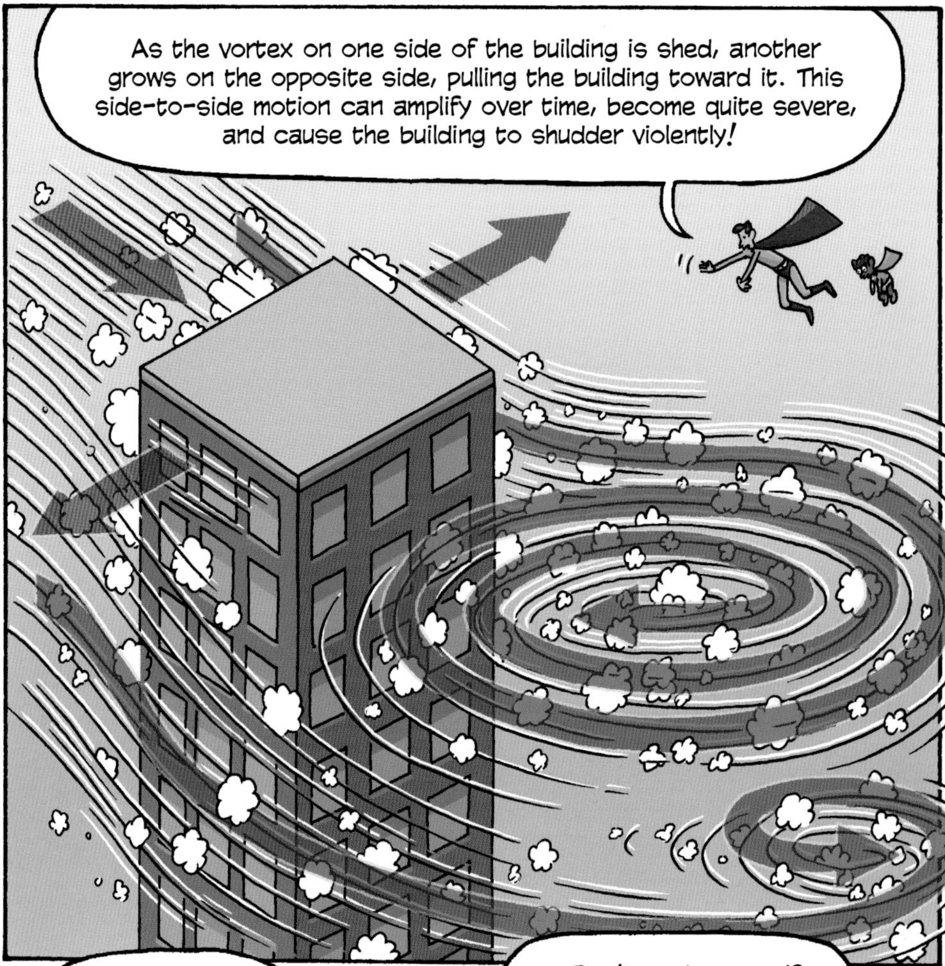
As the vortex on one side of the building is shed, another grows on the opposite side, pulling the building toward it. This side-to-side motion can amplify over time, become quite severe, and cause the building to shudder violently!

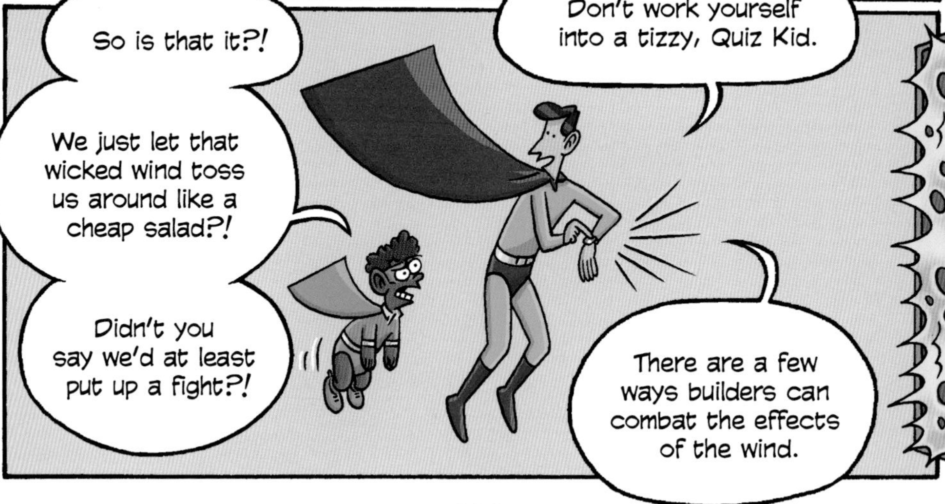
So is that it?!
We just let that wicked wind toss us around like a cheap salad?!
Didn't you say we'd at least put up a fight?!
Don't work yourself into a tizzy, Quiz Kid.
There are a few ways builders can combat the effects of the wind.

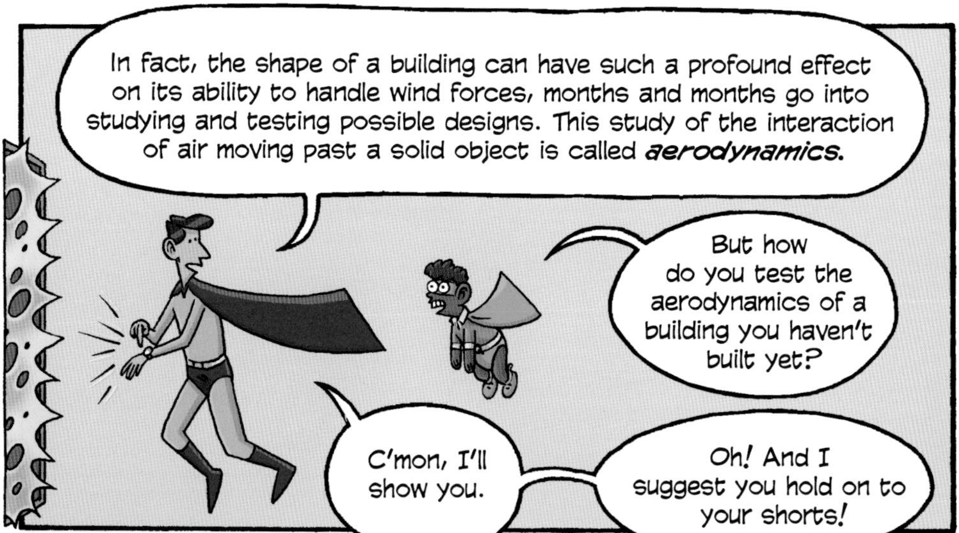
In fact, the shape of a building can have such a profound effect on its ability to handle wind forces, months and months go into studying and testing possible designs. This study of the interaction of air moving past a solid object is called ***aerodynamics.***
But how do you test the aerodynamics of a building you haven't built yet?
C'mon, I'll show you.
Oh! And I suggest you hold on to your shorts!

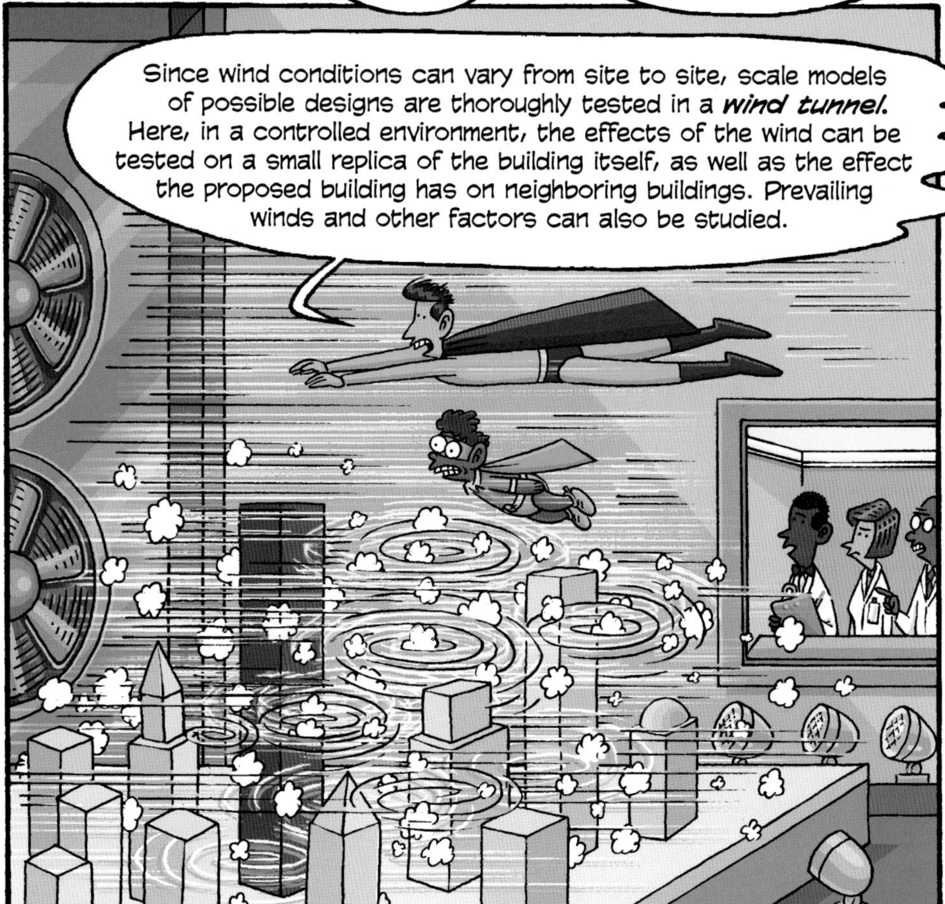
Since wind conditions can vary from site to site, scale models of possible designs are thoroughly tested in a ***wind tunnel.*** Here, in a controlled environment, the effects of the wind can be tested on a small replica of the building itself, as well as the effect the proposed building has on neighboring buildings. Prevailing winds and other factors can also be studied.

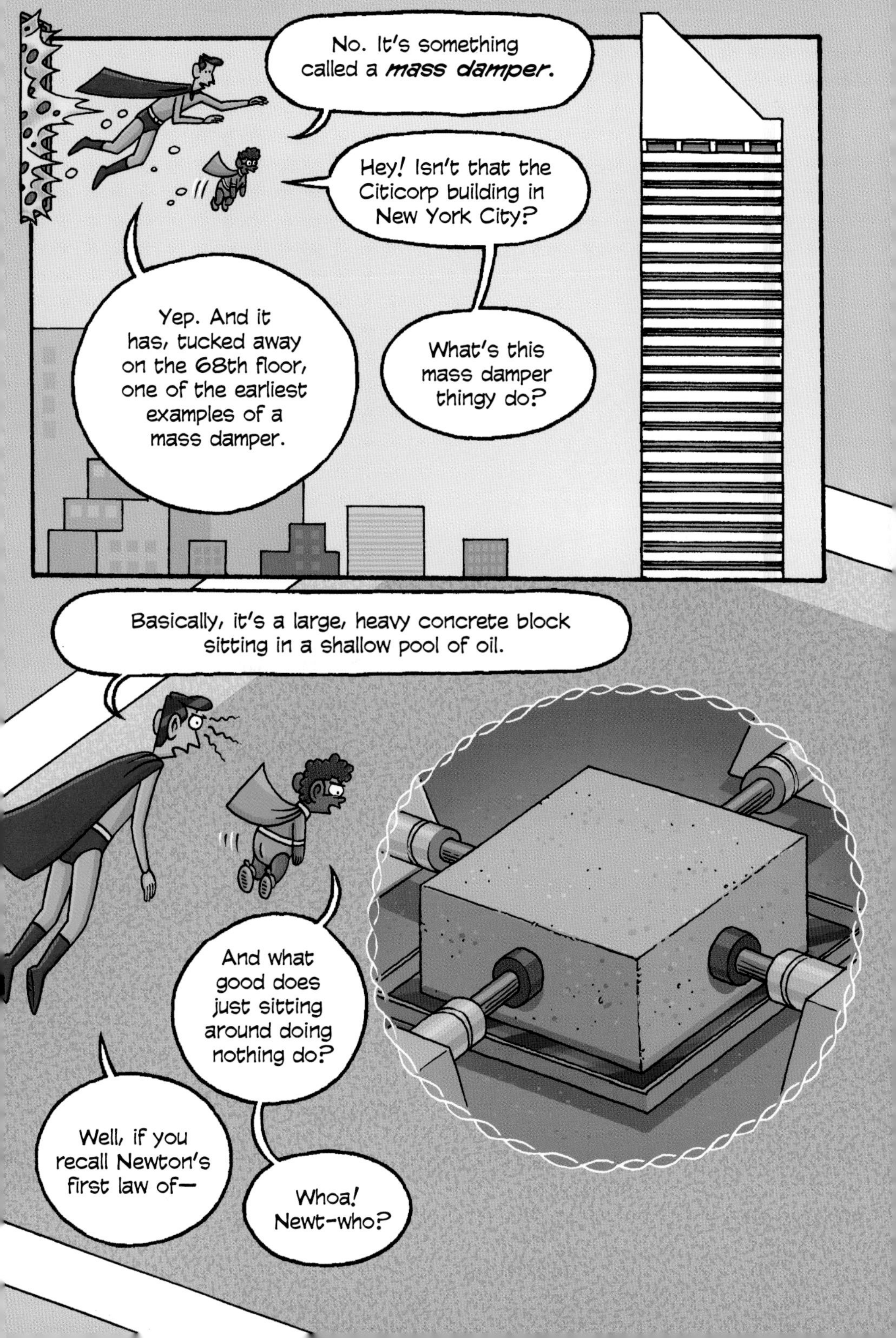
No. It's something called a *mass damper.*
Hey! Isn't that the Citicorp building in New York City?
Yep. And it has, tucked away on the 68th floor, one of the earliest examples of a mass damper.
What's this mass damper thingy do?
Basically, it's a large, heavy concrete block sitting in a shallow pool of oil.
And what good does just sitting around doing nothing do?
Well, if you recall Newton's first law of—
Whoa! Newt-who?

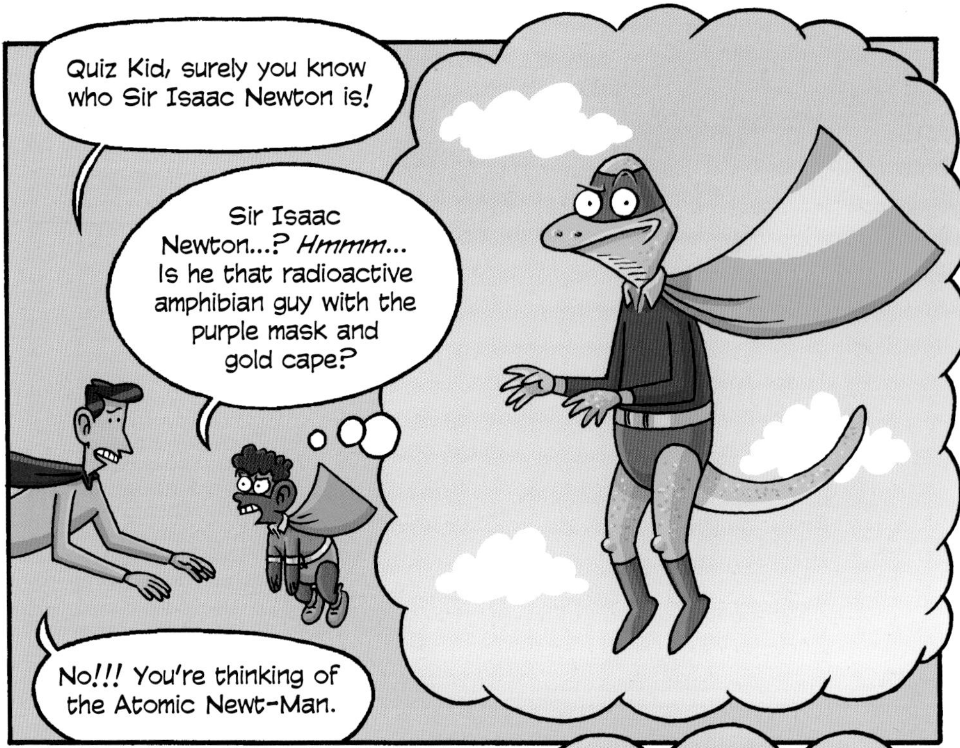
Quiz Kid, surely you know who Sir Isaac Newton is!
Sir Isaac Newton...? *Hmmm...* Is he that radioactive amphibian guy with the purple mask and gold cape?
No!!! You're thinking of the Atomic Newt-Man.

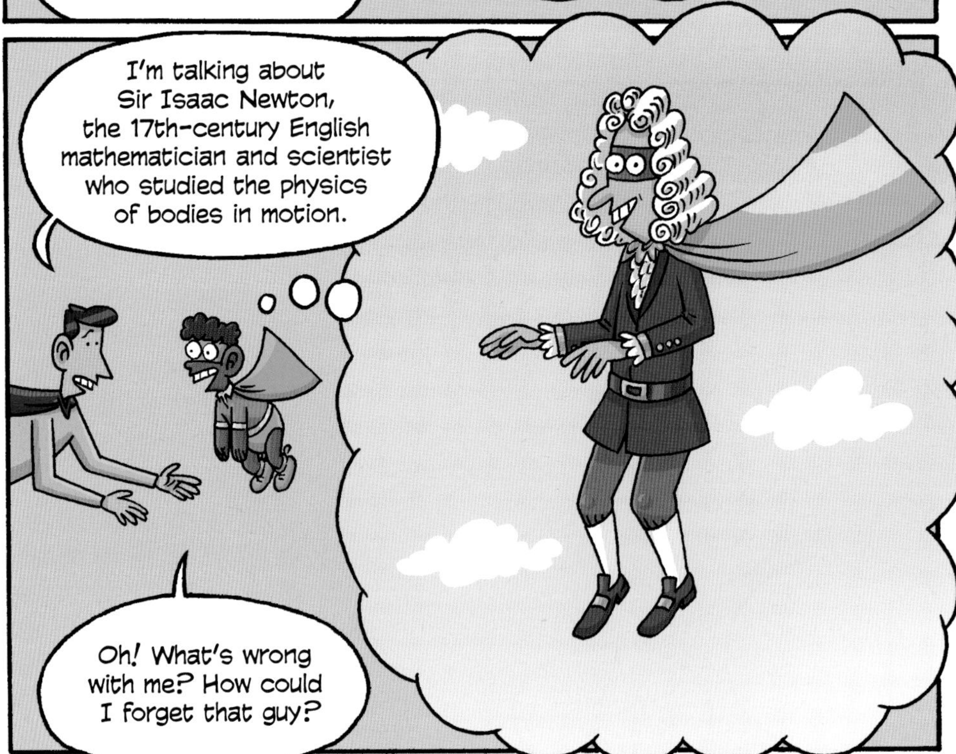
I'm talking about Sir Isaac Newton, the 17th-century English mathematician and scientist who studied the physics of bodies in motion.
Oh! What's wrong with me? How could I forget that guy?

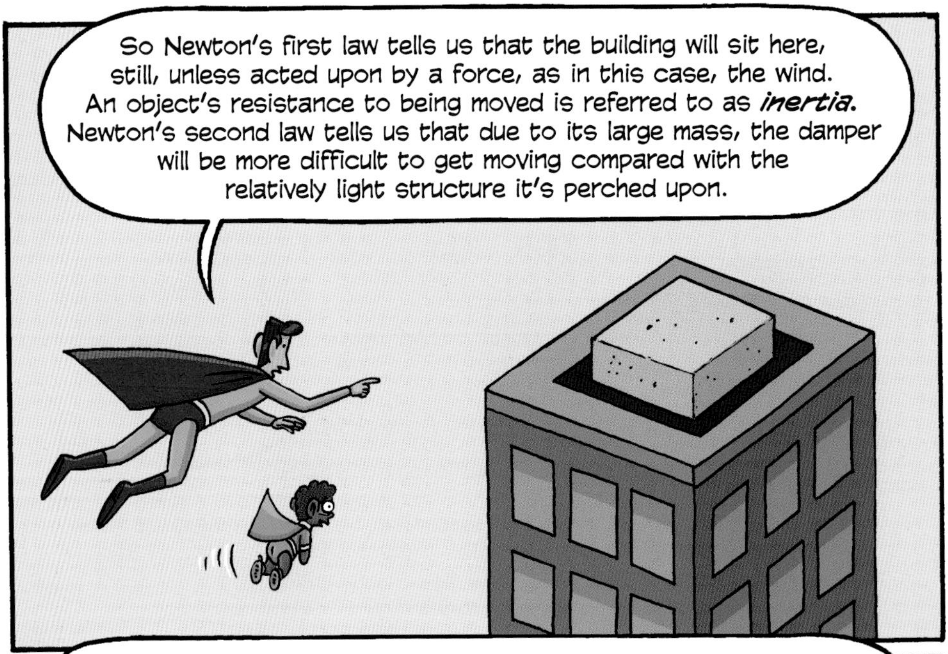
So Newton's first law tells us that the building will sit here, still, unless acted upon by a force, as in this case, the wind. An object's resistance to being moved is referred to as *inertia.* Newton's second law tells us that due to its large mass, the damper will be more difficult to get moving compared with the relatively light structure it's perched upon.

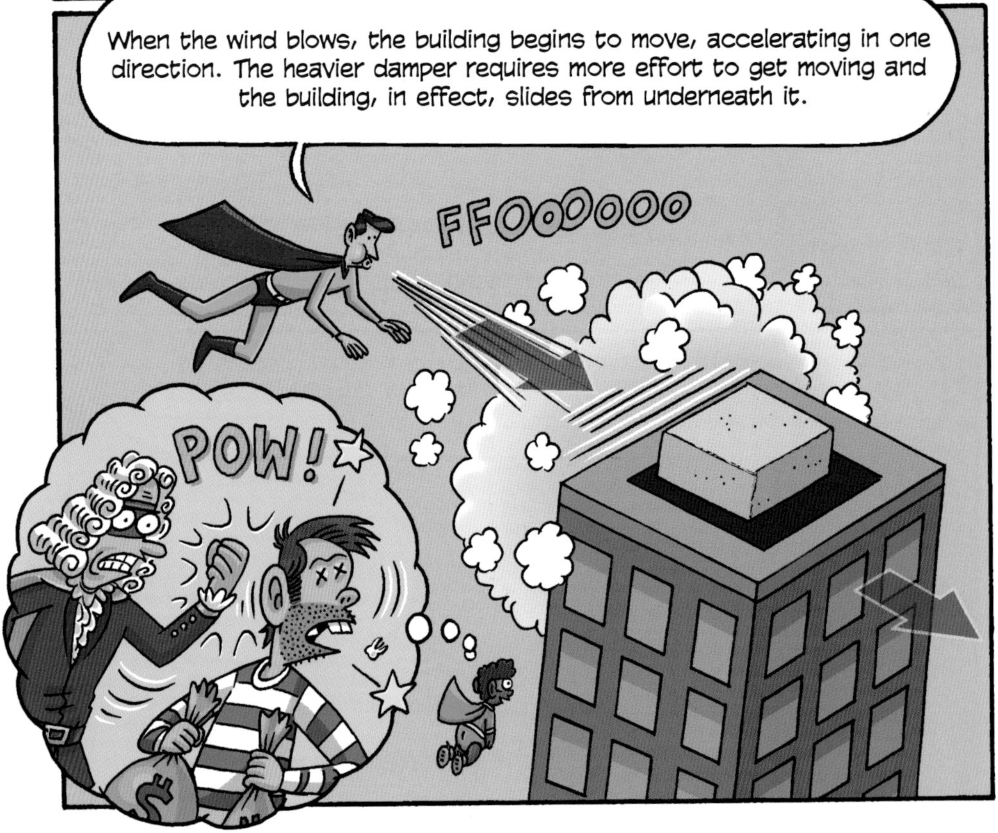
When the wind blows, the building begins to move, accelerating in one direction. The heavier damper requires more effort to get moving and the building, in effect, slides from underneath it.
FFOoOOOO
POW!

The towers of the Bosco Verticale in Italy aren't overwhelmingly tall, but check it out—they're covered in more than 17,000 plants that help clean Milan's air and provide shade and natural insulation for the building.

The 787 ft (239.8 m) tall towers of the Bahrain Trade Center are connected by three skybridges with turbines attached, intended to harness the wind and use it to help power the building.

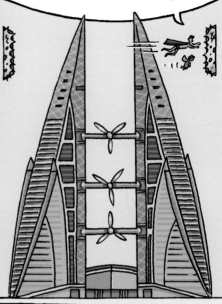

Wowzers! What will they think of next?

Well, unfortunately, my watch doesn't allow us to travel into the future or I'd show you some of what's on the horizon as far as the skyline is concerned.

Uh... Did I mention I was supposed to be home for dinner?

Oh my! And I've missed an entire day at work! I know! I'll set my watch to take us back to the beginning of the day, when we started our little skyscraper adventure.

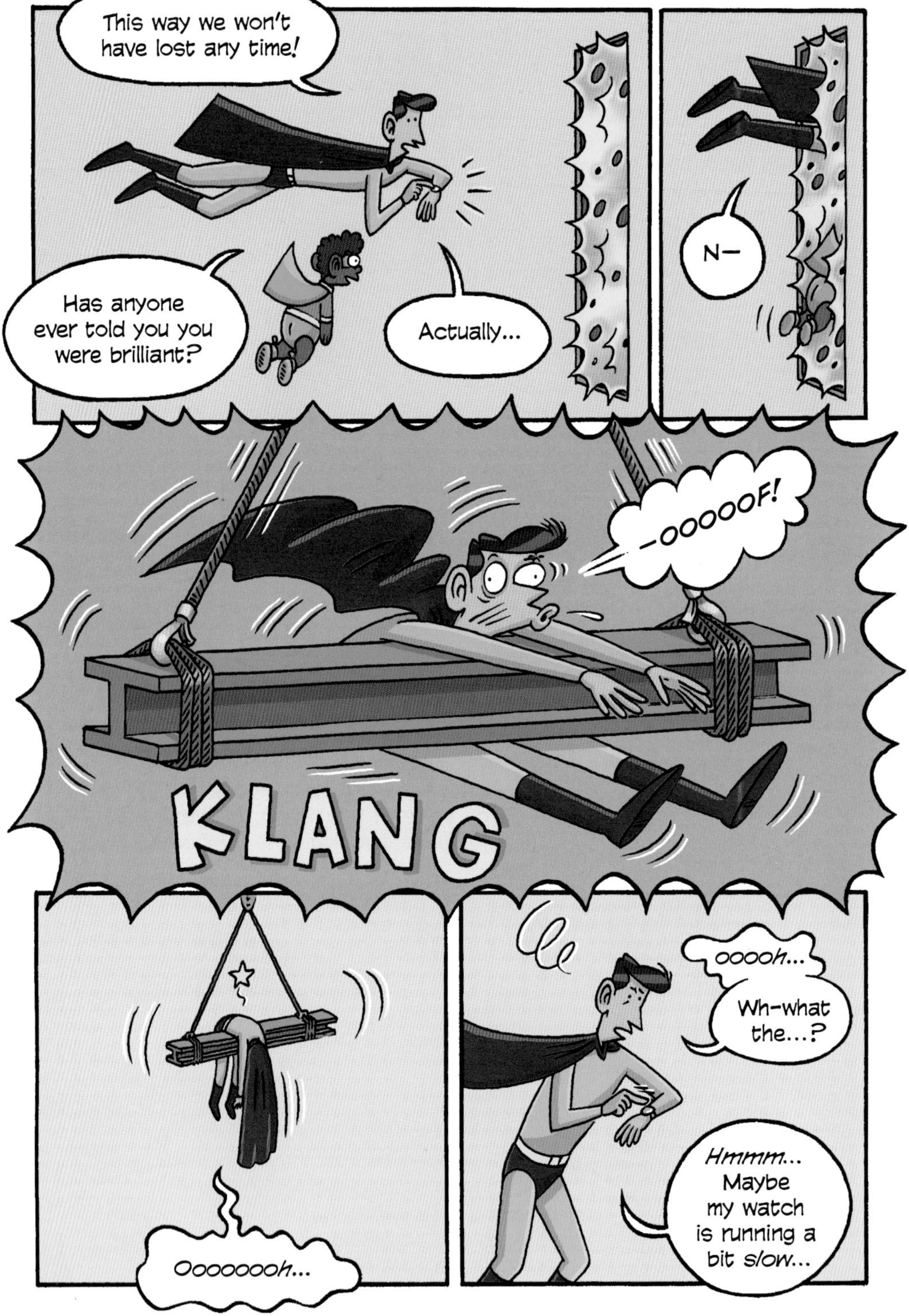
This way we won't have lost any time!
Has anyone ever told you you were brilliant?
Actually...
N—
-OOOOOF!
KLANG
Ooooooh...
ooooh...
Wh-what the...?
Hmmm... Maybe my watch is running a bit *slow*...

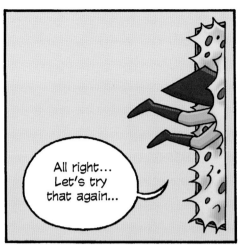

All right...
Let's try
that again...

Hey, Quiz Kid.
Sorry about that.

What took
you so long?

Umm... I'm not sure. I think it's time I took my watch in for servicing. But no big deal! I still have the whole day ahead of me. And so do you, Quiz Kid! Enjoy it! Now I've got to change into my secret-identity disguise and get to work! Gotta pay the bills, y'know!

Say, may
I ask what
you do?

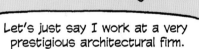

Let's just say I work at a very
prestigious architectural firm.

Anyway, Quiz Kid, it
was really nice to—

Don'tcha
just hate long
goodbyes?

Huh!... What
a curious kid...

SWOOOSH

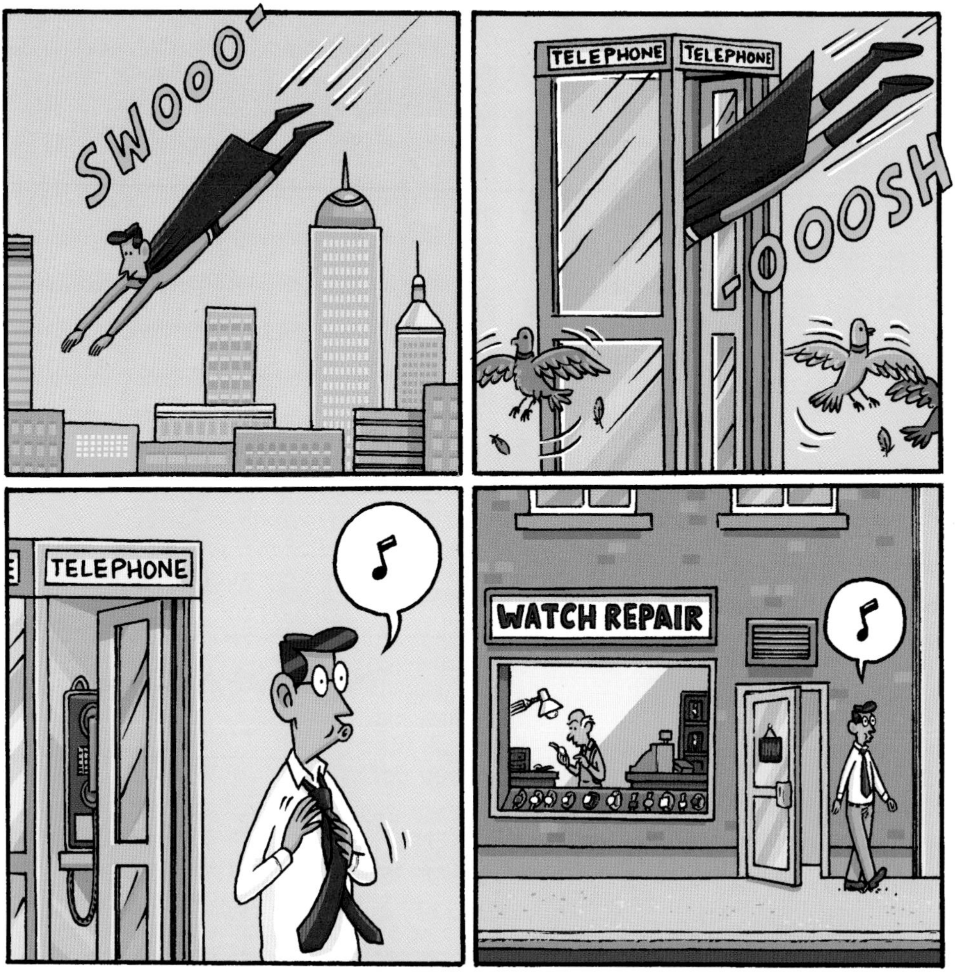
SWOOO
TELEPHONE
TELEPHONE
-OOOSH
TELEPHONE
WATCH REPAIR
AIR

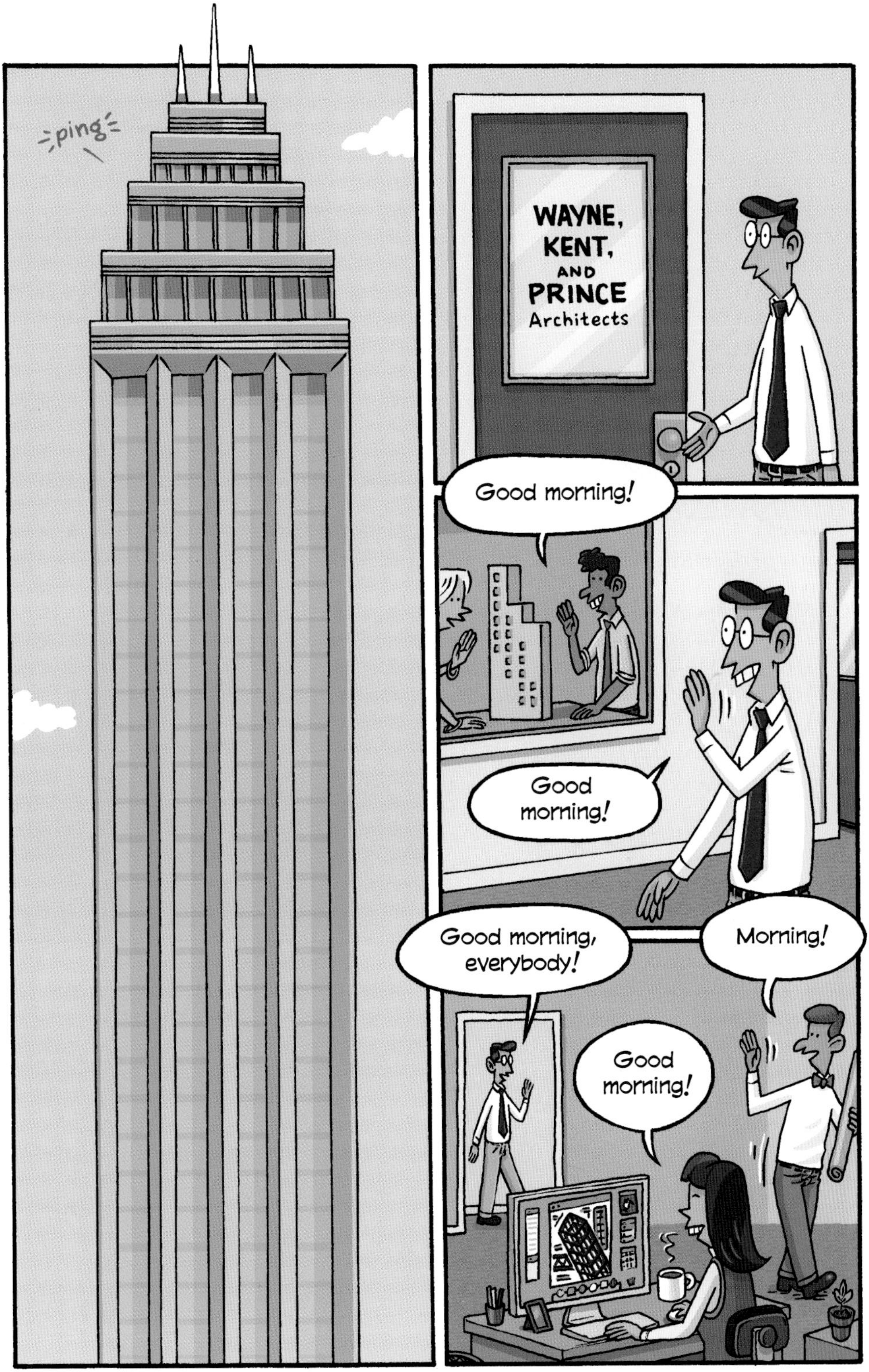
ping
WAYNE, KENT, AND PRINCE Architects
Good morning!
Good morning!
Good morning, everybody!
Morning!
Good morning!

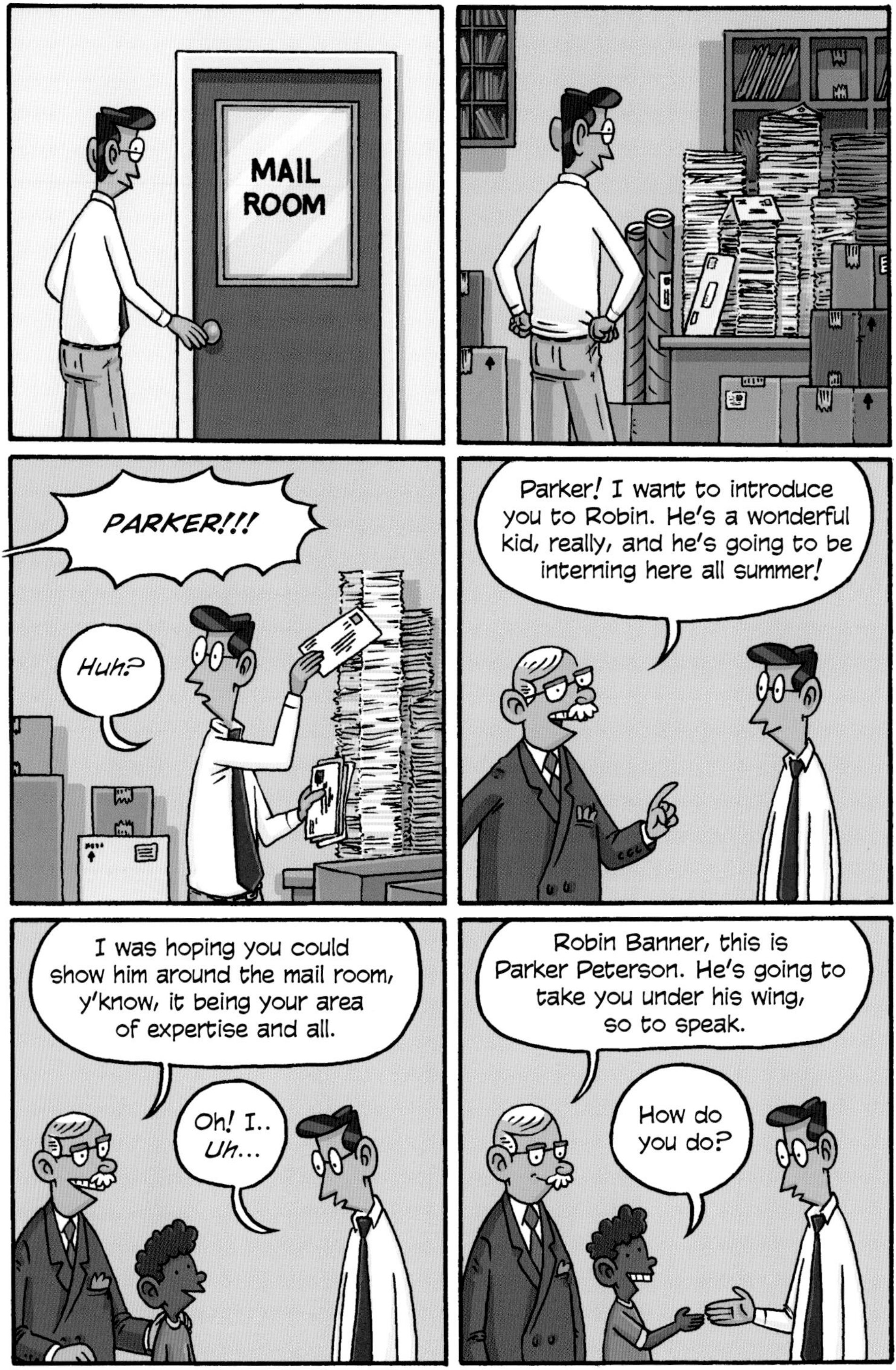
MAIL ROOM
PARKER!!!
Huh?
Parker! I want to introduce you to Robin. He's a wonderful kid, really, and he's going to be interning here all summer!
I was hoping you could show him around the mail room, y'know, it being your area of expertise and all.
Oh! I.. Uh...
Robin Banner, this is Parker Peterson. He's going to take you under his wing, so to speak.
How do you do?